CW00956490

# THE DUCHESS (OF MALFI)

in a new version by
## ZINNIE HARRIS

after John Webster

*The Duchess (of Malfi)* was first performed
at the Royal Lyceum Theatre Edinburgh
on Friday 17 May 2019 as a co-production between the
Royal Lyceum Theatre Edinburgh and Citizens Theatre, Glasgow.

# THE DUCHESS (OF MALFI)

## By Zinnie Harris

### Cast

*in alphabetical order*

| | |
|---:|---|
| **Adam Best** | Bosola |
| **George Costigan** | Cardinal |
| **Eleanor Kane** | Musician |
| **Graham Mackay-Bruce** | Antonio |
| **Fletcher Mathers** | Cariola/Doctor |
| **Angus Miller** | Ferdinand |
| **Kirsty Stuart** | Duchess |
| **Adam Tompa** | Delio |
| **Leah Walker** | Julia |

*Young Company, Edinburgh*
*Lyceum Youth Theatre members*

Luke Davidson, Caleb Dickson, Cariba Falconer,
Stuart Manson, Zack McGlynn, Georgette McMillan,
Lucas Need, Noah Osmani.

## Creative Team

| | |
|---|---|
| Director and Writer | **Zinnie Harris** |
| Designer | **Tom Piper** |
| Composer | **Oğuz Kaplangi** |
| Lighting Designer | **Ben Ormerod** |
| Sound Designer | **MJ McCarthy** |
| Video Designer | **Jamie Macdonald** |
| Movement Director | **Kally Lloyd-Jones** |
| Fight Director | **Renny Krupinski** |
| Dramaturg | **Frances Poet** |
| Casting Director | **Laura Donnelly** CDG |
| Associate Designer | **Max Johns** |
| Assistant Director | **Isla Cowan** |

## Credits

*The Duchess* (*of Malfi*) was made at the Royal Lyceum Theatre Edinburgh; all scenery, props and costumes for this production were made at The Lyceum Workshops at Roseburn, Edinburgh.

Zinnie Harris wishes to thank Ali de Souza, Charlie O'Cover, Jack McCreadie, Guy Hodgkinson, Calvin Noble, Arturo Martinez Vazquez, Yingxue Zhang, Rebecca Gunn, Felixe Forde, Alanah Jackson, Fran and Mark Shaw, Neil Rhodes, Jem Birrell.

# CAST

### ADAM BEST | Bosola

**Theatre appearances:** *Long Day's Journey into Night* (Royal Lyceum Theatre Edinburgh); *Crime and Punishment* (Citizens Theatre/Royal Lyceum Theatre Edinburgh/Liverpool Everyman); *The Oresteia – This Restless House* (Citizens Theatre); *Hedda Gabler* (National Theatre of Great Britain/UK tour); *Twelfth Night, The Plough and the Stars* (National Theatre of Great Britain); *Lions and Tigers* (Shakespeare's Globe); *Flare Path* (Original Theatre Company).

**Television, Film and Radio:** *Giri/Haji*, *The Little Stranger*, *Death of a Salesman*.

Adam trained at Royal Welsh College of Music and Drama.

### GEORGE COSTIGAN | Cardinal

George Costigan first worked on The Lyceum stage in 2003 playing Claudius in Calixto Bieto's production of *Hamlet*. He returned ten years later in 2013 in Dominic Hill's Glasgow Citizens production of Chris Hannan's version of *Crime and Punishment* and most recently in Zinnie Harris's adaptation of *The Oresteia – This Restless House*. George has appeared on television in *Happy Valley* and also appears in this year's *Gentleman Jack*, both written and directed by Sally Wainwright. Film work includes *The Hawk*, directed by David Hayman, and *Summer*, directed by Kenny Glenaan. His trilogy of novels *The Single Soldier* and *The Soldier's Home* was published last year.

### GRAHAM MACKAY-BRUCE | Antonio

**Theatre appearances:** *Jack and the Beanstalk* (Eden Court); *Travesties, Chicago, Scrooge* (Pitlochry Festival Theatre); *The Last Witch* (Pitlochry Festival Theatre/Tron Theatre/ Traverse Theatre); *Brigadoom* (Oran Mor); *No Way to Treat a Lady* (Landor Theatre); *Scrooge* (National tour); *The Tempest* (Italian tour); *A Christmas Carol* (Byre Theatre); *Cinderella* (Sheffield Lyceum); *Sleeping Beauty* (Eden Court); *La Cage aux Folles* (English Theatre, Frankfurt); *My Fair Lady* (Perth Rep); *Hard Times* (Union Chapel); *Late and Lyrical* (Jermyn Street Theatre); *Les Miserables* (Palace Theatre); *The Phantom of the Opera* (Her Majesty's Theatre).

**Television and Film:** *Boheme*, *Specsavers*, *Follow My Lead*.

**Other credits:** Graham performed at the following concerts: *Les Miserables* (Windsor Castle), soloist in *Masters of the House* (touring) and *West End International* (Paris).

Graham trained at Royal Academy of Music.

**FLETCHER MATHERS | Cariola/Doctor**

**Theatre appearances:** *Stiff*, *Whisky Galore* (Royal Lyceum Theatre Edinburgh); *Hamlet* (Citizens Theatre); *First Snow* (National Theatre of Scotland/Theatre Pap/Montreal/Hotel Motel, Montreal); *Two*, *Death and the Maiden*, *Dr Sullivan and Mr Gilbert*, *Retreat*, *Macbeth* (Mull Theatre); *The Reason I Jump*, *Shift*, *To Begin* (National Theatre of Scotland); *Girlfriends* (Oldham Coliseum/ Playhouse Theatre, London); *Private Lives* (Byre Theatre); *The Greenhouse Effect* (Leatherhead Theatre); *The 306 Day* (National Theatre of Scotland/ Stellar Quines).

**Television, Film and Radio:** *Shetland*, Dani's *House*, *Crossroads*, *Govan Ghost Story*, *End of Story.*

**Other credits:** Fletcher toured America with the Pasadena Roof Orchestra as their lead female vocalist/dancer and she is the Project Director of Limelight Music, a company which changes people's lives through music. She co-wrote the Tron Theatre's highly successful pantomimes for five years and is an experienced voice-over artist – she has been the on-board announcer for all Scotrail trains for fourteen years.

Fletcher trained at the Royal Scottish Academy of Music and Drama.

**ANGUS MILLER | Ferdinand**

**Theatre appearances:** *The Belle's Stratagem* (Royal Lyceum Theatre Edinburgh); *Trainspotting* (Citizens Theatre/Selladoor); *Pandemonium* (Prunecchio International Arts Festival); *Let the Right One In* (National Theatre of Scotland/Marla Rubin Productions/Bill Kenwright); *Pink Confetti* (Babel Performing Arts Festival); *Bulldog* (Etch); *Macbeth* (Horsecross Arts).

**Television and Film:** *Shetland*, *Teacup Travels*, *Crowman.*

Angus trained at Drama Centre London.

**KIRSTY STUART | Duchess**

**Theatre appearances:** *Infamous Brothers Davenport* (Royal Lyceum Theatre Edinburgh/Vox Motus); The *Oresteia – This Restless House* (Citizens Theatre/ National Theatre of Scotland); *Fever Dream: Southside* (Citizens Theatre); *Gut* (Traverse Theatre/National Theatre of Scotland); *Crude*, *Spring Awakening* (Grid Iron); *The Girl in the Machine* (Traverse Theatre, Breakfast Plays); *Flo*, *Thoughts Spoken Aloud From Above*, *Tristan Nightaway* (Oran Mor); *Uncanny Valley* (Ayr Gaiety/Edinburgh Science Festival); *Molly Whuppie*, *Licketyleap* (Licketyspit); *The Silence of Bees* (The Arches); *The Hunted* (Visible Fictions); *Romeo and Juliet* (Open Book); *I Was a Beautiful Day* (Finborough/Tron Theatre); *Fast Labour* (West Yorkshire Playhouse/Hampstead).

**Television, Film and Radio:** *Call the Midwife*, *Shetland*, *Outlander*, *River City*, *Lip Service*, *Doctors*, *Sea of Souls*, *Closing the Ring*, *Keeping Mum*, *Cry Babies.*

Kirsty trained at Drama Centre London.

### ADAM TOMPA | Delio

**Theatre appearances:** *Cockpit*, *The Hour We Knew Nothing of Each Other* (Royal Lyceum Theatre Edinburgh); *Macbeth without Words*, *Ubu Roi*, *LOVE*, *Forbidden Stories* (Ludens Ensemble); *Wilds*, *U (You) for Utopia* (Indie).

**Other credits:** Adam is a collaborator of Ludens Ensemble with whom he developed four multi-media physical shows. He has also recently become a co-founder of Edinburgh Physical Theatre Lab.

Adam trained at the University of Theatre and Film Arts Budapest, Hungary.

### LEAH WALKER | Julia

**Theatre appearances:** *Lord of the Flies* (Sherman/Theatr Clwyd); *Hamlet*, *Jane Eyre* (Bolton Octagon); *Ode To Leeds* (West Yorkshire Playhouse); *Amédée* (Birmingham REP); *The Skriker* (Manchester Royal Exchange); *The Sam Wanamaker Festival* (Shakespeare's Globe).

**Television:** *Citizen Khan*, *In The Dark*, *The Dumping Ground*, *Obsession Dark Desires*, *The Evermoor Chronicles*, *Safe*, *Invaders*, *Lucky Man*, *The Royals*.

Leah trained at Liverpool Institute of Performing Arts (LIPA).

### ELEANOR KANE | Musician

**Theatre appearances:** *Billionaire Boy* (Nuffield Southampton Theatres City/UK tour); *Fun Home* (Young Vic); *Threeway* (Edinburgh Fringe); *Werther* (Theatre Royal/Scottish Opera).

# CREATIVE TEAM

**ZINNIE HARRIS | Writer & Director**

**Theatre credits:** Writing credits include her adaptation of *Rhinoceros* (Royal Lyceum Theatre Edinburgh); *This Restless House* (Citizens Theatre/National Theatre of Scotland); *Meet Me At Dawn* (Traverse Theatre); *How To Hold Your Breath*, *Nightingale and Chase* (Royal Court Theatre); *The Wheel* (National Theatre of Scotland); *Further than the Furthest Thing* (National Theatre of Great Britain/Tron Theatre); *Midwinter, Solstice* (RSC); *Fall* (Traverse Theatre/RSC); *By Many Wounds* (Hampstead Theatre); *A Doll's House* (Donmar Warehouse). Directing credits include *A Number* (Royal Lyceum Theatre Edinburgh); *Gut* (Traverse Theatre/National Theatre of Scotland); *Tracks of the Winter Bear* (Traverse Theatre); *The Garden* (Sound Festival); *Midwinter, Solstice* (RSC); *Gilt* (7:84); *Dealers Choice* (Tron Theatre).

**Television:** *Partners in Crime, Spooks, Richard Is My Boyfriend, Born with Two Mothers.*

**Other credits:** Zinnie Harris received an Arts Foundation Fellowship for playwriting and was writer-in-residence with the RSC (2000–01).

**Awards:** Zinnie has received multiple awards including the Peggy Ramsay Award, John Whiting Award and several Fringe First Awards. She was joint winner of the 2011 Amnesty International Freedom of Expression Award, won the CATS award for Best Director for her production of *A Number* at the Royal Lyceum Theatre Edinburgh, and Best New Play for *This Restless House*.


**TOM PIPER | Designer**

**Theatre credits:** *Rhinoceros* (Royal Lyceum Theatre Edinburgh); *Hay Fever* (Royal Lyceum Theatre Edinburgh/Citizens Theatre); *Endgame, King Lear, Hamlet, The Libertine, Nora* (Citizens Theatre); *Cyrano de Bergerac* (National Theatre of Scotland/Royal Lyceum Theatre Edinburgh/Citizens Theatre); *Pelléas Et Mélisande, Eugene Onegin* (Garsington Opera); *Frankenstein, Hedda Gabler* (Northern Stage); *iHo* (Hampstead Theatre); *Harrogate* (HighTide/Royal Court); *A Midsummer Night's Dream, Romeo and Juliet* (Royal Shakespeare Company/UK tour); *Carmen La Cubana* (Le Chatelet, Paris); *White teeth* (Kiln); *Red Velvet* (West End/Tricycle Theatre/New York); *A Wolf in Snakeskin Shoes* (Tricycle Theatre); *The King's Speech* (Birmingham REP/Chichester Festival Theatre/UK tour); *Orfeo* (Royal Opera House); *Tamburlaine The Great* (Theatre for a New Audience, New York).

**Other credits:** Tom designed *Blood Swept Lands* and *Seas of Red* at the Tower of London and received an MBE for services to Theatre and First World War commemorations. Other recent exhibitions include: *Dr Blighty* (Nutkhut, 14–18 NOW); *Curtain Up* (V&A, Lincoln Centre New York); *Shakespeare Staging the World* (British Museum).

He was Associate Designer at the RSC for ten years and has designed over thirty productions for the company.

**Awards:** Tom won an Olivier Award for Best Costume Design for *The Histories* (RSC). He also received an award for Best Design, CATS, for *Twelfth Night* (Dundee Rep).

### OĞUZ KAPLANGI | Composer

**Theatre credits:** *Rhinoceros* (Royal Lyceum Theatre Edinburgh/DOT Theatre, Istanbul/Edinburgh International Festival); *Let the Right One In* (Zorlu PSM/DOT Theatre, Istanbul); *#WeAreArrested* (RSC, Stratford upon Avon); *Meet Me at Dawn* (DOT Theatre, Istanbul).

**Awards and Nominations:** Oguz won the award for the Best Music and Sound at the Critics for Theatre in Scotland 2018 and was nominated for Best Stage Music at the Afife Theatre Awards 2017.

### BEN ORMEROD | Lighting Designer

**Theatre credits:** *A Number* (Royal Lyceum Theatre Edinburgh); *This Restless House, Hamlet, King Lear* (Citizens Theatre)*; The Libertine, Mrs Henderson Presents, Onassis, Macbeth, Legal Fictions, Zorro!* (West End); *The Tempest* (Print Room); *Trouble in Mind, The One That Got Away, Things We Do For Love, Intimate Apparel* (Bath); *Donegal, You Never Can Tell, She Stoops to Conquer* (Abbey Theatre); *The Death of a Comedian, The One* (Soho Theatre); *The Herbal Bed* (Theatre Clwyd); *Fings Aint Wot They Used T'be* (Stratford East); *The Colleen Bawn* (Druid); *In The Next Room or the Vibrator Play* (St James); *The Beauty Queen of Leenane* (Druid/West End/Broadway/ Sydney/Toronto); *The Crucible* (Lyric, Belfast); *Dimetos* (Donmar Warehouse).

**Other credits:** Opera includes *Tannhäuser, Tristan und Isolde, Der Ring des Nibelungen* (Longborough); *Casse Noisette* (Grand Théâtre Genève); *La Traviata* (Danish National Opera). Dance includes *The Happiness Project* (Umanoove); *Three Dancers* (Ballet Rambert); *See Blue Through* (Ballet Gulbenklan/Phoenix Dance).

Ben is also lighting designer for the Calico Museum of Textiles, Ahmedabad, directed Athol Fugard's *Dimetos* (Gate, London) and adapted four films from Kieslowski's *Dekalog* for E15.

### MICHAEL JOHN McCARTHY | Sound Designer

**Theatre credits:** *Wendy and Peter Pan, The Hour We Knew Nothing of Each Other, Glory on Earth, A Number, The Weir, Bondagers* (Royal Lyceum Theatre Edinburgh); *Nora: A Doll's House, Trainspotting, The Gorbals Vampire, Rapunzel, Into That Darkness, Fever Dream: Southside, Sports Day*

(Citizens Theatre); *What Girls Are Made Of*, *Ulster American*, *Gut*, *How to Disappear*, *Grain in the Blood* (Traverse Theatre); *Pride & Prejudice\* (\*Sort Of)* (Blood of the Young/Tron Theatre); *God of Carnage*, *The Lonesome West*, *Under Milk Wood* (Tron Theatre); *Jimmy's Hall* (Abbey Theatre); *Rocket Post*, *In Time O' Strife*, *The Tin Forest*, *The Day I Swapped My Dad for Two Goldfish* (National Theatre of Scotland); *A*ugust: *Osage County*, *George's Marvellous Medicine*, T*he Cheviot*, *the Stag and the Black*, *Black Oil*, *The BFG*, *Steel Magnolias* (Dundee Rep); *Light Boxes*, *Letters Home*, *The Authorised Kate Bane* (Grid Iron).

### JAMIE MACDONALD | Video Designer

**Theatre credits:** *The Arabian Nights*, *Alice's Adventures in Wonderland*, *The BFG* (Royal Lyceum Theatre Edinburgh); *Mammy Goose*, *Chimera* (Tron Theatre); *Submarine Time Machine* (National Theatre of Scotland); *Warriors*, *The Legend of Slim McBride* (Scottish Opera Education); *The Little Mermaid* (Macrobert); *Wendy Hoose* (Random Accomplice/Birds of Paradise); *The Legend of Slim McBride*, *Curse of the MacCabbra Opera House*, *Way Out West* (Scottish Opera Education); *From Here* (Lyra Theatre); *But Why?*, *Project Branded*, *The Woolgatherers*, *Multiplex* (Tron Skillshops); *News Just In*, *The Incredible Adventures of See-Thru Sam* (Random Accomplice).

**Awards and Nominations:** Jamie won the Best Technical Presentation award twice for his work on *Alice's Adventures in Wonderland* and *Incredible Adventures of See-Thru Sam* at the Critics' Awards for Theatre in Scotland. He also received a Nomination for Best Technical Presentation for his work on *Wendy Hoose* at the Critics' Awards for Theatre in Scotland.

Jamie trained at Duncan of Jordanstone College of Art and Design, Dundee.

### KALLY LLOYD-JONES | Movement Director

**Theatre credits:** Movement Director credits include *Cyrano de Bergerac* (National Theatre of Scotland/Royal Lyceum Theatre Edinburgh/Citizens Theatre); *Rigoletto* (Scottish Opera); *Die Fledermaus* (RCS); *Jenufa* (Danish National Opera/Royal Swedish Opera); *Madame Butterfly* (Glyndebourne Opera); *I Puritani* (Gran Liceu, Barcelona); *Love and Information* (Solar Bear/RCS). Choreographer credits include *The Belle's Stratagem* (Royal Lyceum Theatre Edinburgh). Directing credits Include *Cavalleria Rusticana* (Edinburgh Grand Opera); *Lauder* (Jamie MacDougall/Scottish Opera); *Grace Notes* (Scottish Opera); *Le Vin Herbé* (RCS); *Hansel and Gretel* (RCS/St Magnus International Festival). Dance credits include *The Chosen*, *Lady Macbeth: Unsex Me Here*, *Nijinsky's Last Jump*.

**Awards:** Kally received the Herald Angel Award for Directing *The Seven Deadly* Sins and the Sunday Herald Culture Award for Best Live Performance for *Lady Macbeth: Unsex Me Here.*

**RENNY KRUPINSKI | Fight Director**

**Theatre credits:** *Cyrano de Bergerac* (National Theatre of Scotland/Royal Lyceum Theatre Edinburgh/Citizens Theatre Glasgow); *The Provoked Wife*, *The Hypocrite*, *The Winter's Tale*, *The Merry Wives of Windsor*, The Shoemaker's Holiday, *Twelfth Night* (RSC); *Jane Eyre* (National Theatre); *Coriolanus*, *King Lear* (Shakespeare's Globe); *Imagine This*, *Making Noise Quietly*, *The Postman Always Rings Twice*, *Backbeat*, *Crazy For You* (London West End); *Twelfth Night* (Young Vic); *Shakespeare In Love* (National tour); *True West*, *King Lear* (Citizens Theatre Glasgow); *The Ladykillers* (Theatre by the Lake); *One Flew Over the Cuckoo's Nest*, *Julius Caesar*, *Lady Chatterley's Lover* (Sheffield Crucible); *Cyrano de Bergerac*, *Romeo and Juliet*, *Macbeth* (Theatr Clwyd); *Treasure Island*, *Khandan* (Birmingham Rep); *A Short History of Tractors in Ukrainian*, *Jack Lear* (Hull Truck).

**Television and Film:**,*Emmerdale*, *Coronation Street*, *Hollyoaks*, *Rownd a Rownd*, *So Awkward*, *Man Like Mobeen*, *Blue Murder*, *Jamaica Inn*, *West is West*, *Greyhawk*, *The Crossing*, *Tyrannosaur*.

**Other credits:** Renny wrote and directed *A Dangerous Woman*, *Bare*, *Katie Crowder*, *Lady Macbeth Rewrites the Rulebook*, *The Alphabet Girl*, *D'Eon*. *D'Eon* will be produced in Athens in November 2019. Renny also wrote many BBC Radio 4 comedies and *The Bill* for three years.

**Awards and Nominations:** Renny was nominated as Best Actor by *The Stage*, won a Darkchat Best Director award and received a Scotsman Fringe First for his play *Bare*. He also won a *Manchester Evening News* award for Best Supporting Actor as Wemmick in *Great Expectations* at The Royal Exchange Manchester.

**FRANCES POET | Dramaturg**

**Theatre credits:** Writing credits include *Gut* (Winner of Writers Guild Best Play Award, Traverse Theatre/National Theatre of Scotland); *Adam* (Winner of Fringe First, Herald Angel and Scottish Arts Club Awards, Traverse Theatre/ MacRobert Arts Centre/Citizens Theatre); *The Macbeths* (Circle Studio, Citizens Theatre); *Dance of Death* (Circle Studio/Citizens Theatre); *What Put the Blood* (Abbey Theatre); *Andromaque* (Orán Mòr/Byre Theatre, St Andrews); *The Misanthrope* (Orán Mòr); *Faith Fall* (Orán Mòr/Bristol's Tobacco Factory).

Frances is a Glasgow-based writer with eighteen years' experience working as a dramaturg for leading British theatres. Frances is currently Literary Associate at the Citizens Theatre.

**LAURA DONNELLY** CDG | **Casting Director**

**Theatre credits:** *Jumpy*, *Alice's Adventures in Wonderland*, *Wendy and Peter Pan*, *Cyrano De Bergerac Twelfth Night*, *Rhinoceros*, *The Arabian Nights*, *The Winter's Tale*, *Hay Fever*, *Glory on Earth*, *Cockpit* (Royal Lyceum Theatre

Edinburgh); *Lampedusa* (Citizens Theatre); *This Restless House* (Citizens Theatre/National Theatre of Scotland/Edinburgh International Festival); *Midsummer* (National Theatre of Scotland/Edinburgh International Festival); *My Left Right Foot* (National Theatre of Scotland/Birds of Paradise); *First Snow* (National Theatre of Scotland/Theatre Pap/Hotel Motel); *Eddie and the Slumber Sisters* (National Theatre of Scotland/Catherine Wheels); *Adam, How To Act* (National Theatre of Scotland); *The 306 Trilogy: Dawn, Day, Dusk* (National Theatre of Scotland/Perth Theatre); *Our Ladies Of Perpetual Succour* (National Theatre of Scotland/Live/ Sonia Friedman/UK tours, National Theatre/Duke of York's); *The James Plays* (National Theatre of Scotland/National Theatre/Edinburgh International Festival, UK/International); *The Strange Undoing of Prudencia Hart* (New York Residency/US tour); *Let the Right One In* (US Tour/Abbey Theatre Dublin); *Anything That Gives Off Light* (National Theatre of Scotland/The TEAM/Edinburgh International Festival).

Laura is the Current Casting Director at National Theatre of Scotland.


## MAX JOHNS | Associate Designer

**Theatre credits:** *Wendy and Peter Pan* (Royal Lyceum Theatre Edinburgh); *Utility, Twelfth Night* (Orange Tree Theatre); *Buggy Baby* (The Yard); *Yellowman* (Young Vic); *Under a Cardboard Sea, Life Raft, Medusa* (Bristol Old Vic); *Baddies* (Synergy Theatre Project); *There Shall Be Fireworks* (The Plasticine Men); *Enron, Our Town, The Eleventh Hour* (The Egg); *Kes* (Leeds Playhouse); *Hamlet, All's Well That Ends Well, Noisy Nativity, Strawberry and Chocolate* (Tobacco Factory Theatres); *The Half God of Rainfall* (Fuel/Kiln/Birmingham Rep); *Strange Fruit* (The Bush); *Rust* (The Bush/HighTide); King John (RSC).

**Other credits:** *Fidelio* (London Philharmonic Orchestra).

Max trained at the Bristol Old Vic Theatre School, and won a BBC Performing Arts Fellowship Award in 2015.


## ISLA COWAN | Assistant Director

**Theatre credits:** Assistant Director credits include *Success* (Royal Lyceum Theatre Edinburgh); *GUT* (National Theatre of Scotland/Traverse Theatre); *Ben-Hur* (Reading Rep). Playwright credits include *The View from 2038* (Royal Lyceum Theatre Edinburgh); *These Walls* (Sweet Venues); *Nibble Nibble Gnaw* (Dundee Rep STRIPPED). Director and Playwright credits include *Lily* (Corpus Playroom); *Come Back to Bed* (Fitzpatrick Theatre).

**Awards:** *Waiting* (Best Play, DDS New Writing Festival, 2017).

Isla studied English Literature at the University of Cambridge and a Master's in Writing for Performance at the University of St Andrews.

ARTISTIC DIRECTOR **DAVID GREIG**
EXECUTIVE DIRECTOR **MIKE GRIFFITHS**

**The Royal Lyceum Theatre Edinburgh is the leading producing theatre in
Scotland and one of the United Kingdom's most prolific theatre companies.**

Our beautiful, intimate Victorian theatre was built in 1883 and has played
a significant role in the cultural and creative life of the city and surrounding area
for over 130 years. Since 1965, the current Lyceum company has developed a
reputation for innovative, high-quality theatre, drawing upon the considerable
talent in Scotland as well as developing award-winning work with partners across
the globe to make theatre in Edinburgh that can speak to the world.

We believe that making and watching theatre together is life enhancing. We are
committed to being a theatre rooted in our community, a truly civic theatre
entertaining, challenging and inspiring all the people of Edinburgh. To reach the
widest possible audience we find new ways to open our doors and stage to the
public, as well as reaching out into Edinburgh's schools and neighbourhoods with
a range of programmes taking place beyond our walls.

Season 2018/19 saw the company stage new production of *Twelfth Night*, *Cyrano
de Bergerac*, a Scottish premiere of *Wendy and Peter Pan*, and three world
premieres: *Touching the Void*, an acclaimed adaptation based on Joe Simpson's
memoir by David Greig; *The Duchess (of Malfi)* in a new version by Zinnie Harris;
and sell-out stage musical *Local Hero*, a critically acclaimed adaptation of the
classic Scottish film with book by Bill Forsyth and David Greig, and new music and
lyrics by Mark Knopfler. *Local Hero* will play at The Old Vic, London in Spring
2020. Last year The Lyceum's production of *Pressure* by David Haig ran at The
Ambassadors Theatre in the West End.

For the latest information about The Lyceum visit **lyceum.org.uk**

For a full Royal Lyceum Theatre Edinburgh staff list please visit
**lyceum.org.uk/staff**

ALBA | CHRUTHACHAIL

THE CITY OF EDINBURGH COUNCIL

Royal Lyceum Theatre Company is a Scottish Charity
Registered No. SC010509

# CITIZENS THEATRE

ARTISTIC DIRECTOR **DOMINIC HILL**
EXECUTIVE DIRECTOR **ALEX MCGOWAN**

*The Duchess (of Malfi)* **is part of the Citizens Women season, a year dedicated to showcasing the extraordinary and wide-ranging talent of women theatre-makers.**

The Citizens Theatre is Glasgow's major producing theatre and one of the leading theatre companies in the UK. Over the last 75 years, the Citizens has built an international reputation for producing innovative shows on stage, alongside a highly regarded learning programme of participatory and education work. Led by Executive Director Alex McGowan and Artistic Director Dominic Hill, who is regarded as having 'a talent for classical drama which is genuinely world class' (*Daily Telegraph*), it presents bold new interpretations of classic texts that are accessible and relevant – and, uniquely, where any member of the audience can attend a performance for as little as 50p.

We believe in breaking down barriers to engagement with the arts and that everyone should have the opportunity to take part. Throughout the year we offer a range of opportunities for people of all ages and backgrounds to get involved in the creative life of our theatre.

Our beautiful Victorian home in the Gorbals is currently closed while it undergoes a major redevelopment. This will be the first comprehensive, integrated redevelopment of the building in its 140-year history. The project will transform the experiences of audiences, participants and performers and secure the future of one of Scotland's most iconic buildings and leading producing theatres. During the redevelopment, our shows will be presented at Tramway and across Scotland with classes and activities based at Scotland Street School Museum.

For the latest information about the Citizens Theatre visit **citz.co.uk**

For a full Citizens Theatre staff list please visit **citz.co.uk/staff**

ALBA | CHRUTHACHAIL

Citizens Theatre is a Scottish Charity Registered No. SC001337

# The Duchess (of Malfi)

Zinnie Harris's plays include the multi-award-winning *Further than the Furthest Thing* (National Theatre/Tron Theatre; winner of the 1999 Peggy Ramsay Award 2001, John Whiting Award, Edinburgh Fringe First Award), *How to Hold Your Breath* (Royal Court Theatre; joint winner of the Berwin Lee Award), *The Wheel* (National Theatre of Scotland; joint winner of the 2011 Amnesty International Freedom of Expression Award), *Nightingale and Chase* (Royal Court Theatre), *Midwinter*, *Solstice* (both RSC), *Fall* (Traverse Theatre/RSC), *By Many Wounds* (Hampstead Theatre) and the trilogy *This Restless House*, based on Aeschylus' *Oresteia* (Citizens Theatre/National Theatre of Scotland; Best New Play, Critics Award for Theatre in Scotland). Also Ibsen's *A Doll's House* for the Donmar Warehouse, Strindberg's *Miss Julie* for the National Theatre of Scotland, and (*Fall of*) *The Master Builder* for Leeds Playhouse. She received an Arts Foundation Fellowship for playwriting, and was Writer in Residence at the RSC, 2000–2001. She is Professor of Playwriting and Screenwriting at the University of St Andrews, and was the Associate Director at the Traverse Theatre 2015–2018.

ZINNIE HARRIS

# The Duchess
# (of Malfi)

*in a new version after*
JOHN WEBSTER

FABER & FABER

First published in 2019
by Faber and Faber Ltd
74–77 Great Russell Street
London WC1B 3DA

Typeset by Country Setting, Kingsdown, Kent CT14 8ES
Printed in England by CPI Group (UK) Ltd, Croydon CR0 4YY

© Zinnie Harris, 2019

The right of Zinnie Harris to be identified as author
of this work has been asserted in accordance with Section 77
of the Copyright, Designs and Patents Act 1988

A CIP record for this book
is available from the British Library

978-0-571-35538-9

2 4 6 8 10 9 7 5 3 1

The Duchess (of Malfi) was first performed at the Royal Lyceum Theatre Edinburgh on 17 May 2019. The cast, in alphabetical order, was as follows:

**Bosola**  Adam Best
**Cardinal**  George Costigan
**Musician**  Eleanor Kane
**Antonio**  Graham Mackay-Bruce
**Cariola / Doctor**  Fletcher Mathers
**Ferdinand**  Angus Miller
**Duchess**  Kirsty Stuart
**Delio**  Adam Tompa
**Julia**  Leah Walker

*Director*  Zinnie Harris
*Designer*  Tom Piper
*Associate Designer*  Max Johns
*Lighting Designer*  Ben Ormerod
*Composer*  Oguz Kaplangi
*Sound Designer*  M. J. McCarthy
*Dramaturg*  Frances Poet
*Assistant Director*  Isla Cowan
*Casting Director*  Laura Donnelly

# Characters

The Duchess

The Cardinal

Ferdinand

Antonio

Bosola

Julia

Cariola

Delio

Executioners

Doctor

Musician

# THE DUCHESS
# (OF MALFI)

*For Pauline Knowles*

# Note on Punctuation

The spoken lines in this text start with a lower-case letter to stop lines reading like a statement; lines are often incomplete phrases, half-thoughts or utterances that pass from one to another, and are rarely whole sentences.

In general the spoken text is laid out according to each character's process of reasoning with each new line indicating a new thought.

# Act One

## ONE: THE DUCHESS

*A Woman stands alone on a large stage.*

*She steps forward.*

*She looks out to the audience.*

*She puts her hands in front of her eyes and peers.*

*She starts to hum.*

*Someone brings her a microphone.*

**Woman**  thank you

*She takes the microphone into her hand.*

*She takes a breath, she is about to sing.*

*A guitar strums a note.*

*She stops, she looks around.*

*The lights change around her. A drum gently joins in.*

*She starts to sing. It's a song that feels familiar – stand nearer, breathe deeper, it's the heat of night . . . talk longer, move slower, hold me tight . . .*

*She is just starting to find her confidence, to enjoy the song, when the world changes. The sides of the stage seem to close in on her.*

*Two men come on to the stage.*

*Whatever that was, it had the feeling of a dream.*

**Ferdinand**  sister

**Cardinal** we wish to speak to you –

*She looks at them.*

**Duchess** when did you arrive?

**Cardinal** you are a widow now

**Duchess** yes

**Cardinal** and a duchess, and of course royalty

**Ferdinand** high blood, respected

**Duchess** we all are

**Cardinal** and no doubt you're thinking your mourning is behind you but –

**Ferdinand** a word of caution

**Cardinal** let's not let good looks, eloquence and sweet-talking

**Ferdinand** turn our heads

*She looks at her brothers, not sure she is following.*

**Duchess** my head has not turned –?

**Cardinal** because people that dally around, we always think –

**Duchess** dally around?

**Ferdinand** marry again

**Cardinal** it's like they are soiled goods, no? Their livers spotted

**Ferdinand** over-used

**Cardinal** you are a jewel of utter beauty, of course, but – jewels actually *lose* their value when they've been bought and sold

**Ferdinand** yes, to pass through many hands produces a sort of tarnishing

**Duchess**  don't diamonds gain value that way?

**Ferdinand**  but that means whores would be precious –

**Duchess**  I'm not thinking about marrying again
so if that's your worry –

**Cardinal**  a lot of widows say that but, after a month or
two, you seem changed already –

**Duchess**  I'm exactly the same

**Cardinal**  what we mean is, you live in comfort here,
don't you? In the court, there is a kind of honey dew, our
family has status and you are attractive

**Ferdinand**  men will come with open faces and say
anything to get in your –

**Cardinal**  watch out, dear sister! It could be poison –

**Ferdinand**  two-faced swine are more like witches in
disguise

**Cardinal**  and yes the devil lurks beneath their skins.

**Duchess**  this is such wise counsel –

**Ferdinand**  oh sarcasm, yes, very witty

**Cardinal**  and you can throw us off but in the end
everything you do, even your most private thoughts

**Ferdinand**  some weddings are said to be executed rather
than celebrated

**Cardinal**  the marriage night an entrance to some prison

**Ferdinand**  and will the pleasure

**Cardinal**  the carnal pleasure

**Ferdinand**  seem so sweet after the domestic dungeon has
shut its doors?

*The Duchess looks at them.*

*She puts her tea down.*

*She looks at them again.*

*She laughs a bit.*

**Ferdinand**  what are you doing?

*She laughs a bit more.*

**Cardinal**  stop that.

*She laughs harder.*

**Duchess**  I'm sorry it is just –

*She carries on laughing. Then she really laughs.*

**Ferdinand**  you're an insult, you know that

*She continues to laugh.*

**Cardinal**  oh please just stop it.

*She stops it.*

*She picks up a teacup and laughs even more into it.*

**Ferdinand**  I told you she'd be like this

**Cardinal**  sister, you have to listen to us –

**Ferdinand**  look we brought you something

**Cardinal**  we know officially you no longer need to wear black
  but we thought –

*They show her the dress. Grey and drab.*

*She looks at it.*

*She laughs even harder.*

can you stop her?

**Ferdinand**  can you suggest how?

*She laughs again.*

*They put the dress down.*

*The Cardinal catches her by the hand.*

**Cardinal**  sister, please, you are the closest thing we have. And we are worried.

**Duchess**  don't be worried

**Cardinal**  we used to feel we knew you

**Duchess**  I was a mouse

**Ferdinand**  you were who you had always been

**Duchess**  in a cage

**Cardinal**  we were in Naples, they'd heard of you there

**Ferdinand**  in the square, sitting, we heard these men talking

**Duchess**  good

**Cardinal**  how can you say that, they knew we were nearby and still they were going on –

**Duchess**  I'm not afraid of people talking about me

**Ferdinand**  you don't want to know what they were saying?

**Duchess**  was it nice things?

**Cardinal**  of course it wasn't

**Duchess**  well never mind

**Ferdinand**  you're courting attention

**Duchess**  of course I'm not

**Ferdinand**  the young and wanton duchess. Looking for an adventure, and why not she has got all this money now

**Duchess**  oh stop it

**Ferdinand**  that outfit

**Duchess**  what outfit?

**Cardinal**  the way you walk

**Ferdinand**  the way you flaunt

**Duchess**  I don't flaunt, what do I flaunt?

*Beat.*

**Cardinal**  listen, we are all a little more stirred up than we intended

**Duchess**  did you plan this whole thing, it feels kind of rehearsed?

*Beat.*

**Cardinal**  we only want to protect you

**Duchess**  be happy for me,
   I'm a widow yes but I have a chance to live again. I am still young. Hooray.
   I am not going to wear grey. And stay indoors.
   no, sorry.
   now will you stay for something to eat or not?

*They look at each other.*

**Cardinal**  I can't stay

**Duchess**  really, brother?

**Cardinal**  I have to get back. I have an appointment this evening

**Duchess**  well, I wish you would come here with a smile just once. Both of you.

*She kisses Ferdinand. She kisses the Cardinal.*

*The Cardinal leaves.*

*The Duchess and Ferdinand look at each other.*

so was this his idea or yours?

**Ferdinand** you know we have a point

**Duchess** I was married to a bore, Ferdinand

**Ferdinand** a wealthy duke

**Duchess** he was a barnacle
he was so flimsy, I can't tell you

**Ferdinand** he was rich

**Duchess** tedious and sombre
and in bed, I hate to say all force no fancy

**Ferdinand** whoa –

**Duchess** I'm sorry if I am not sad enough or seemly
enough but really –

**Ferdinand** whoa whoa whoa
I wish you wouldn't talk like this

**Duchess** just be happy for me then?

**Ferdinand** yes, happy, but we worry also.
you're my little sister, if I can't worry then –

**Duchess** hang on – little sister?

**Ferdinand** yes, little

**Duchess** but by seconds I am the older

**Ferdinand** ahh yes. But by my sex I am the stronger

**Duchess** okay but I am the richer

**Ferdinand** I am more powerful

**Duchess** more powerful? no
I have three houses now, to your one

**Ferdinand** I am a man
   that trumps you, you're a woman

**Duchess** ah but I am the Duchess

*He stands up to her. For a second his face can't be read.*

**Ferdinand** so you are
   goodnight then, duchess

**Duchess** is this a game? I can't tell if you're mucking
about –
   I was playing, right?

**Ferdinand** goodnight.

*Beat.*

**Duchess** Ferdinand? Honestly I was only –

*He walks out.*

**Duchess** oi. Come back.
   we always play –

*He has gone.*

damn

*The Duchess looks at herself in the mirror.*

*Moves some hair out of her eyes.*

*Looks again.*

*Looks at her contours.*

what do you think, Cariola?
   is this what I should wear?

*She holds up the grey dress to herself.*

**Cariola** what?

**Duchess** cover myself and look drab?

**Cariola**  yuk, why would you do that?

**Duchess**  is it my money or my shape that's more dangerous?

*The Duchess puts the dress down.*

*Cariola helps her get ready for bed.*

*The wind blows.*

**Duchess**  goodness, it's wild out there –

**Cariola**  shall I shut the window, madam?

**Duchess**  no, I like it.
    the restlessness suits me.
    send my steward in

*Cariola raises an eyebrow.*

**Cariola**  really?

**Duchess**  I have a question for him.

**Cariola**  I am sure, and he an answer.

*Antonio knocks.*

**Duchess**  oh
    yes, hello

**Antonio**  you called for me?

**Duchess**  well, it was –
    I want to know what I am worth –

**Antonio**  what do you mean, worth?

**Duchess**  you're my book-keeper, you know about assets don't you?

**Antonio**  what assets are we talking about?

**Duchess**  all assets

**Antonio**  I'm not sure I understand

**Duchess**  I'm just wondering what I have to my name?

**Antonio**  well, you have plenty, do you really want to talk about this now?

**Duchess**  yes

**Antonio**  in your room?

**Duchess**  I happen to be in my room and so, well, we might as well talk about it now, but –

**Antonio**  you're in your nightie

**Duchess**  well yes, I am in my nightie but
if I own so much how can I trust those around me?

**Antonio**  madam?

**Duchess**  Antonio?

**Antonio**  what?

**Duchess**  you know what –

**Antonio**  well, where is everyone?

**Duchess**  gone

**Antonio**  sure?

**Duchess**  yes

*He looks about.*

**Antonio**  alright
well

*He comes over and taps her on the arm.*

your assets are fine.
it's nice to see them

*He puts an arm on her shoulder, but only briefly.*

**Duchess**  so much?

**Antonio**  actually seriously
   if we are talking about your accounts, you took on
three more staff this week

**Duchess**  I was hoping for a kiss

*He kisses her.*

*But it's short, a peck.*

**Duchess**  again

**Antonio**  is it such a good idea? In your room at this time
of night

**Duchess**  you didn't mind yesterday

**Antonio**  that was a one-off

**Duchess**  let's have a second-off

*She kisses him passionately.*

my family is closing in, I might not be able to do this
tomorrow.

**Antonio**  what if someone sees us?

**Duchess**  who is going to see us?

**Antonio**  you have fourteen servants

**Duchess**  tchhh
   anyway I have fifteen servants, what do you mean,
fourteen?

**Antonio**  well, I wasn't counting –

**Duchess**  yourself?
   well, that is a mistake.
   you are the most servanty of all.

*She pulls at Antonio's shirt.*

alright, if you insist on actually doing my accounts, take
pen and ink, write:

**Antonio**  what now?

**Duchess**  yes, steward, are you ready?

**Antonio**  yes

**Duchess**  let's do an audit.

*Antonio takes a pen.*

**Antonio**  an audit?

*He puts his shirt back up.*

**Duchess**  no leave it.

*The Duchess puts her face into Antonio's back and breathes in.*

so, first column. What am I, and to whom?
  write it down

**Antonio**  well . . . you have three houses

**Duchess**  it's true I have three houses

**Antonio**  six horses

**Duchess**  pff

**Antonio**  a fortune in the bank

*She comes up to him.*

*He drops his pencil for a second.*

**Duchess**  traditionally aren't a woman's assets shared with her husband?

**Antonio**  traditionally yes

**Duchess**  so as my husband died we can't account for these things

**Antonio**  do you want me to start another column?

**Duchess**  unless I remarry

**Antonio**  heavens, this is a strange audit

**Duchess**  you started it

**Antonio**  no, it was you

**Duchess**  perhaps you could list me the advantages

**Antonio**  of what?

**Duchess**  of marriage, that is what we are talking.

**Antonio**  are we?

**Duchess**  should I take a husband? New page, let's make a table in your book

**Antonio**  okay

**Duchess**  first one
  I could choose someone nice, better than last time

**Antonio**  yes, excellent

**Duchess**  but what about him, what would he give me?

**Antonio**  hmm. That would depend who you chose

**Duchess**  one of your eyes is bloodshot

**Antonio**  I've been working too late, I rubbed it

**Duchess**  use my ring to fix it

**Antonio**  old wives' tale

**Duchess**  it works, a wedding ring cures lots of things
  I said I would never take it off until I gave it to someone I loved

**Antonio**  but you're giving it to me

**Duchess**  to help your eyesight

**Antonio**  it's actually made me blinder

**Duchess**  what?

*She takes the ring and looks in it.*

oh, there is a saucy and ambitious devil dancing in this
circle, that's why
    remove him –

**Antonio** how?

**Duchess** with your finger
    poke him out

**Antonio** put my finger through this wedding band?

**Duchess** does it fit?

**Antonio** don't tease me

**Duchess** who said I am teasing?
    marry me

**Antonio** what?

**Duchess** yes. It makes perfect sense –

**Antonio** now wait a second

**Duchess** why not?

**Antonio** because you aren't being serious,

**Duchess** of course I am

**Antonio** I'm your book-keeper

**Duchess** you're more than you think. A book-keeper yes,
but –

**Antonio** you don't know what you are saying, you
wouldn't marry me

**Duchess** why wouldn't I?
    I love you.
    and the fact that you don't think I would makes you
all the more lovely.

*She kisses him.*

**Antonio** why though, I'm nothing?

**Duchess** not to me.

*She kisses him again.*

**Duchess** only you should know: I sing at parties, I wear colourful dresses, I'm impulsive, headstrong, I won't wear my hair up because you say I should, or do this because you prefer it, in fact I might do the other just to be contrary, I need to work, use my head, I get drunk I swear a lot I lose things all the time but I will be utterly and always myself.

**Antonio** and wonderfully so.

*They kiss again.*

**Duchess** so let's not complicate what should be straight-forward.

*She starts to put the ring on his finger, he pulls it back.*

**Antonio** your brothers –

**Duchess** we won't tell them. We won't tell anyone for a while
    you'll be my husband here only in my room.

**Antonio** and outside?

**Duchess** still my servant, for now.

*He looks at her.*

*He puts a hand to her cheek.*

**Antonio** a secret wedding?

**Duchess** can you bear it?

*She puts the ring on him.*

it's already on your finger, it's too late

**Antonio**  I will be everything you need me to be, I'll talk when you want and be trustworthy, and attentive

**Duchess**  I know

**Antonio**  and will laugh at everything, even if I don't find it funny, actually especially if I don't find it funny and when your feet are cold and wet in winter –

**Duchess**  Antonio?

**Antonio**  yes?

**Duchess**  you can kiss me now

*He kisses her again.*

*His glasses fall off.*

**Antonio**  sorry

*They both laugh.*

*Her maid Cariola appears.*

**Duchess**  we're getting married

**Cariola**  you're mad

**Duchess**  witness it for us, will you

**Cariola**  if I do, it is an absolute contract

**Duchess**  last chance, any doubts?

**Antonio**  she's right, you're mad, you realise, you have lost your head

**Duchess**  I know. Utterly.

*She gets a book and throws it at Cariola.*

read it out

**Cariola**  bless heaven this sacred Gordian which let violence never untwine, are you sure?

**Duchess**  keep going

**Cariola**  and your own sweet affections, like the spheres
be still in motion

**Duchess**  hurry up

**Cariola**  okay, and quickening and make the like soft
music
    it's quite nice language, don't you think? Okay, not
interested
    blah blah, okay here
    man and wife.

*They kiss.*

**Antonio**  that's it?

**Cariola**  well once you have signed, and technically you
are supposed to consummate –

**Antonio**  what does that mean?

**Cariola**  fuck each other's brains out

**Antonio**  very good

**Duchess**  excellent

**Cariola**  can you wait at least until I have left the room –

**Antonio**  I doubt this service would have been prettier if
it had been in a church

**Duchess**  let me put kisses in your hair instead of flowers.

**Cariola**  I never know whether you are more ruled by
a spirt of greatness or of woman

**Antonio**  greatness

**Duchess**  woman

**Cariola**  fearful madness

**Antonio**  love

**Duchess**  determination

**Antonio**  triumph

**Duchess**  don't worry, Cariola, stop frowning

**Cariola**  I am not worried, but heavens, lady!

**Duchess**  there are days for caution and days to throw it back at the wind.
    what do you want me to do, wait and let my brothers trap me into another loveless match? Or worse, hide myself away forever?

**Antonio**  dear love?

**Duchess**  yes

**Antonio**  you said, we had to make this binding.

*Antonio picks up the Duchess and carries her off.*

*She squeals in delight. Cariola is left wondering the sense in all of this.*


## TWO: THE CARDINAL

*The Cardinal is standing in his office. A woman, Julia, is with him.*

**Cardinal**  I don't suppose you'd suck my cock?

*Beat.*

**Julia**  what?

**Cardinal**  surely it's crossed your mind?

**Julia**  what on earth got in to you tonight?

**Cardinal**  sorry, I thought that was what you were thinking. As you were, you came here to ask for absolution, I will write to the Pope. Have we finished now?

**Julia** my husband is here, back in town

**Cardinal** I know, and you love him.

**Julia** you married us

**Cardinal** well at least tell me that you *do* love him and put me out of my misery

*Beat.*

you know I pine for you.

**Julia** you lust for me

**Cardinal** I lust for you, I pine for you, the effect on me is the same

**Julia** I think it will pass

**Cardinal** yes, it will pass, but let's make it pass together

**Julia** you're out of sorts

**Cardinal** is wanting some comfort from you so bad?

**Julia** you're troubled that's all.
a little vein on your forehead is sticking out

*He grabs her.*

**Cardinal** yes, I am troubled, you trouble me
you trouble me very much

**Julia** me?

**Cardinal** let me hold you, please
I'm back to Rome before the end of the week, and Rome is so tedious, let me sustain myself at least with the smell of you

*She holds him.*

say you will be my mistress –

**Julia** I can't

**Cardinal** but why? You sucked my cock once – do it again –

**Julia** listen –

**Cardinal** so what do you intend, to make me sore with longing?

**Julia** of course not

**Cardinal** then think of it this way and that and roundabout the problem. You are here, I am here, what more is there –

**Julia** I only came to ask about the Bible, to tell you that my husband

**Cardinal** your husband your husband
    do you have to talk about him so much?

*Beat.*

I want you to be mine, Julia, is that so bad?

**Julia** but I am taken.

**Cardinal** then don't come here and lift my hopes –

**Julia** the structure we are in
    what is right or wrong, it confuses me

*He comes over to her.*

*He kisses her tenderly.*

**Cardinal** confusion, we can do something about.
    enjoyment and loving is never wrong, there's the answer
    trust me. Okay? And kiss me again?

*He undoes his flies.*

*He takes her head and pushes her down to kneel.*

fucking hell.
    fuck off,

**Julia**  who?

**Cardinal**  someone is watching

**Julia**  where?

*He goes and looks out.*

**Cardinal**  out there,
out the window

**Julia**  what?

**Cardinal**  no don't look
he's mocking me

**Julia**  I can't see him

**Cardinal**  oh because he stands back when you come to
look
it's an image of Christ I think

**Julia**  Christ?

**Cardinal**  yes Christ in rags
sent to scare me
remind me that all this is shallow
precarious
oi, ghost?

**Julia**  I can't see

**Cardinal**  of course you can't
it's a plaything of my mind isn't it
sent for my attention only
some loose connection
guilt or –

**Julia**  who is it?

**Cardinal**  I know who this is, no point even looking, it's
a dead man – a child I knew, grown man now
I had him buried seven years ago

**Julia** for a crime?

**Cardinal** yes murder –
    they strung him up and ripped out his guts
    why am I thinking about him tonight?

*She goes over to the window.*

**Julia** which direction are you looking?

*She looks.*

**Cardinal** I don't believe in angels and demons, so get lost
    oi yes, you ghost
    I looked out for you once but you lost your favour,
    you don't get to haunt me

**Julia** who did he murder?

**Cardinal** he slit throats for a living, how can I remember?
    does it matter? He did what I told him
    but now his ghost thinks he can haunt me
    come away
    oh suck my cock would you please, Julia, and let's be
done with it

**Julia** now?

**Cardinal** why not?
    let's let him see. Do you get your penis sucked in hell,
spirit?
    or are you still too much of a baby to get it up?

*Julia stands next to him.*

*She is about to kneel down.*

**Julia** is that the man you are talking about?

**Cardinal** in the shadows, yes

**Julia** but that's not a ghost

**Cardinal** what?

*He looks.*

**Julia** that's your brother

**Cardinal** Ferdinand?
    well what the hell is he doing here?


### THREE: FERDINAND

*The Cardinal grabs Ferdinand and they go into a bar*

**Ferdinand** what if we were too late in our advice?

**Cardinal** you look drunk –

**Ferdinand** not nearly enough, get me more –

**Cardinal** calm down

**Ferdinand** calm? She was laughing at us when you had gone

**Cardinal** what do you mean?

**Ferdinand** she didn't listen to a word, not one.

**Cardinal** brother –

**Ferdinand** you were hardly out the door when she was talking about how boring her dead husband was in bed.

**Cardinal** no –

**Ferdinand** I fear she is already lost.

**Cardinal** she knows too much about the marriage bed
    you see that's the thing –

**Ferdinand** I went back to the palace, stood outside her room
    the candle is lit in her bedchamber

**Cardinal** for God's sake

**Ferdinand**  she is entertaining

**Cardinal**  I doubt it

**Ferdinand**  she never keeps the candle lit, even when we were children and afraid of the dark –

**Cardinal**  maybe she can't sleep?

**Ferdinand**  she has got someone with her, that is what it means

**Cardinal**  so quickly?

**Ferdinand**  take it from me, we need to do something before this goes too far
  I am her twin, I feel what she feels.
  even the way the breath goes into her body, and tonight –

**Cardinal**  you need to calm yourself.

**Ferdinand**  I think you need to excite yourself. Wake up. she is out of control.
  a conversation here, a wise counsel there. It's nothing.
  she sees herself to be free.
  she sees herself to be in charge

**Cardinal**  she is a widow now, not the unmarried maid we had before –

**Ferdinand**  go and stand outside her window.

**Cardinal**  we have to think with measure this time.

**Ferdinand**  your measure is not for me

**Cardinal**  well, it should be, don't you see your anger is dangerous?

**Ferdinand**  I'm protecting our family. Our position.

**Cardinal**  so am I.

*Beat.*

provided she just entertains then it's no problem, we haven't lost anything

**Ferdinand** I don't care about the money, is it all about the money to you?

**Cardinal** what else is our family but money?

**Ferdinand** people, that is what we are

**Cardinal** exactly, and this town has lots of them
    oi. Bring some water. Cold

**Ferdinand** get off me

**Cardinal** this man needs dunked.

**Ferdinand** away – cretin

**Cardinal** you need to sober up

**Ferdinand** you need to find some fire

**Cardinal** I have plenty fire

**Ferdinand** do something brother. Or fall with her.

*Ferdinand slopes off. One of the people in the bar is watching.*

*Ferdinand snarls at them on the way out.*

*Cardinal watches him go.*

*He drinks something.*

*He thinks about what he has heard.*

*Bosola comes in.*

*The Cardinal looks at him.*

*He puts his drink down.*

**Cardinal** oh, so you do haunt me.

*Bosola grabs the Cardinal and has his head in a vice.*

**Bosola** you can't ignore me –

**Cardinal** get off –

**Bosola** you raised me

**Cardinal** the church raised you, not me, let go

**Bosola** you picked me up from the gutter, fed me, clothed me

**Cardinal** I had you killed

**Bosola** I don't believe it

**Cardinal** believe it

**Bosola** I'm your man, you know I am

**Cardinal** I'll bite you

**Bosola** I'll take it as a sign of affection. I'll bite you back.

*The Cardinal struggles out of his hold.*

**Cardinal** Jesus man, get a grip.

*Bosola lets go of him.*

*The Cardinal looks at him.*

what happened anyway, why aren't you dead?

**Bosola** they sent me on a ship
  I pulled on the oars for six years

**Cardinal** fucking hell. You were supposed to be hanged.

**Bosola** you would have done that?

**Cardinal**  I did, I signed the warrant
   I'll do it again, you lay one hand on me.

**Bosola**  I didn't mention your name, I stayed silent
   I took all the flak

**Cardinal**  you fucked up

**Bosola**  you fucked up

**Cardinal**  but you got caught

**Bosola**  I was loyal

**Cardinal**  you are loyal because you thought your best
chance was with me

**Bosola**  no, I was loyal because I loved you.

**Cardinal**  pffttt.

**Bosola**  you're the only family I have

**Cardinal**  family?

*The Cardinal laughs.*

family? You are a different species, let alone family.
   for God's sake I can smell your breath.

**Bosola**  please let me kiss your ring

**Cardinal**  one step and I will call the guard.
   I am the cardinal, you are a murderer.

**Bosola**  where else can I go, sir?
   If you send me away then where –

**Cardinal**  I'll send you to my brother. You want family. He
has a job.
   get up off your knees. You aren't a child now, stop
snivelling.

*Bosola lets go of him.*

**Bosola**  what job?

**Cardinal** a job that will keep you from starvation. Nothing else.

**Bosola** I knew I could trust you

**Cardinal** my brother is a bastard, you won't thank me


*Bosola and Ferdinand.*

**Bosola** whose throat must I cut?

**Ferdinand** ha, he said you were a thug –

**Bosola** not a thug, a steadfast servant.
  is this honest work?

**Ferdinand** why does it matter what it is?

**Bosola** I prefer honesty now. If there is a choice, I mean. on the ship I had time to think.

**Ferdinand** watching for the truth and reporting it. Is there more honest than that?

**Bosola** the truth is good.
  but there's always a way that the devil gets in.

**Ferdinand** oh, so you're clever? Alright, but no devil. You stay loyal to me.

**Bosola** I'm nothing but loyal, that's my arrow

**Ferdinand** you tell me everything.

**Bosola** in utmost detail

**Ferdinand** can you ride horses by the way, this is harder if you can't

**Bosola** who am I watching?

**Ferdinand** a woman. My twin. You'll be a bishop to her horses

**Bosola** but a spy underneath?

**Ferdinand** in a word, yes, but for her own good. I want to know who she sees and when. Where she goes and when. What she does and when.

**Bosola** I am to be like one of your familiars then –
a little weasel that goes ahead and seeks out

**Ferdinand** do you want it or not?

**Bosola** I need it.
I have no other means of living. The Cardinal knows that.

**Ferdinand** very good. I'll recommend you for the role.

*Beat.*

it's not worth thanks

*Bosola puts his hand out to shake.*

**Bosola** a bishop to her horses? I like it actually. And at my judgement day I will say my corruption grew out of horse dung.

**Ferdinand** anyone ever told you your voice is irritating?

**Bosola** that was a joke only

**Ferdinand** it was my joke first, the bishop was my pun

**Bosola** you're like me then, enjoy the comfort of words

**Ferdinand** take your hand away

**Bosola** why? I'm your creature now

**Ferdinand** what do you mean, 'creature'?

**Bosola** servants take on the outer form of their masters didn't you know? Like a boy grows from his father, a flower from a seed. Indeed as you have a slight lean to your body, and walk like there is a rod up your . . . spine, without being aware of it, before long I would have that stance myself, and as you stay up on your toes, more like a woman than a man in truth but before long I will start, look like this, or actually see your hair is that sickly flame, and nose too long, well, soon you watch I too – will walk like you and talk and think in just your way – and if you are given to spending money on let's say women or men perhaps because I am not one to judge but –

## FIVE: THE MAID

*In the Duchess's house, entrance hall. Cariola is putting on her make-up.*

**Cariola**  you talk too much

**Bosola**  I was a long time silent, I find it makes me a little

**Cariola**  verbose?

**Bosola**  loquacious

**Cariola**  circumlocutory

**Bosola**  periphrastic

**Cariola**  repeating

**Bosola**  I was raised by a man of the church

**Cariola**  where tedious repetition was the order of the day?

**Bosola**  I heard there was a job here

**Cariola**  you heard right

**Bosola**  I have a good record, a reference –

**Cariola**  it's with the horses

**Bosola**  I love horses

**Cariola**  you won't talk them to death?

*Beat.*

**Bosola** I was silent a long time as I told you.
   whenever I am around people, and one like you,
   I find words spew forward like –

**Cariola** boils?

*He smiles.*

**Bosola** boils yes.
   they erupt from my mouth.

*Beat.*

I can't have offended you so easily

**Cariola** offended me? You said I was like a painter,
making a meal of my face. My brush was like a painter's
brush

**Bosola** you have to admit the way you paint that on, you
are like a painter

**Cariola** you said you would sooner eat a dead pigeon
taken from the soles of the feet of the sick of the plague
than kiss someone like me, over-painted and ghastly

**Bosola** perhaps that was a little –

**Cariola** you said the closets of women were more like
shops of witches

**Bosola** I definitely didn't say that –

**Cariola** where you might find the fat of serpents, Jews'
spittle, anything that will cure the face and to what end?

**Bosola** I speak too much.

**Cariola** ahh, but you haven't asked me what I thought
   this is a conversation
   you pose the question *why* do women paint their faces,
but don't listen to the answer. Is it just to cover age? Or

blemishes? could be? or it could be so when we go red to blush or in some other mood, like *violent rage at the misogyny of men around us*, no one but ourselves will know.

*She smiles.*

**Cariola** the steward will be along shortly. Just wait here.

**Bosola** you know, for a woman, I like your wit

**Cariola** I don't care for yours

**Bosola** if you don't like the wit, why wit back?

**Cariola** why indeed.

**Bosola** and so prettily at it.

*Antonio comes in.*

**Antonio** ah, about the horses?

**Bosola** I hear there's a position

**Antonio** where have you come from?

**Cariola** the church he says

**Bosola** I said it was like a church

**Antonio** what did you do there?

**Cariola** pray he says

**Bosola** I said it was like a prayer, I didn't say prayer exactly but silence of one sort

**Antonio** I see

**Cariola** I told him that silence suits the horses well

**Antonio** well, the horses are a little rusty on their prayer but I am sure we can –

**Cariola** what makes a good servant?

**Antonio** what?

**Cariola** you must ask him a question or two, this man is good with wit. Don't just say yes, put him on the spot a little

**Bosola** madam?

**Cariola** play with him, he likes words
  what sort of servant will you be? The steward himself knows that here extra is required, why only this morning tell him you were working hard for the Duchess at an early hour

**Antonio** what?

**Cariola** you kept us all awake
  but not of that, let's give him some space, elaborate
  he talks well, he is garrulous, flowery and rhetorical, let him wit and wind away a while

**Antonio** and the subject?

**Cariola** what makes a man welcome in this household?
  hard work? Loyalty, going the extra mile?

**Bosola** I am loyal

**Cariola** honest?

**Bosola** yes, honesty I put above all else

**Cariola** oh, he is a honest man, put that down, but question him on it, our mistress will want to see what makes a man honest
  why you could even take an hour or two of our time, it seems we have time to kill.

**Antonio** do we?

**Cariola** yes, *grill* him

*Antonio looks at Cariola, not sure what is up.*

*He turns to Bosola.*

**Antonio** go down to the stables and say you were sent by the house.

**Bosola** thank you

**Cariola** so quickly?

**Antonio** aye, go.

*Bosola leaves.*

*Antonio studies Cariola.*

**Cariola** it was just some fun.
  honestly, you never know when to stand forward and when to sit down –

**Antonio** I did stand forward

**Cariola** you let him off far too lightly. He strikes me as a common arsehole of the masculine kind, and we should have rolled him around a little in his own sense of wit.

**Antonio** should we?

**Cariola** yes, we should have. You're the steward here now. A man like that needs to know what is what. Whatever the Duchess sees in her new duke, Antonio, make sure she never sees a mouse.


SIX: ANTONIO

*Antonio sees his old friend Delio.*

**Antonio** am I a mouse?

**Delio** huh?

**Antonio** look at my face

**Delio** I'm looking

*He looks.*

**Antonio** go on –
  you can be honest

**Delio** no

**Antonio** look again

**Delio** what is it?

**Antonio** I need other men to look at me and see a man.
But instead they see this little thing that could be knocked
over in a puff of wind. And don't try and tell me that isn't
so. Every step I think I must step differently, then I look
in the mirror and I think, nothing is different. Exactly
as I was. A tiny timid creature. Or worse, a man but not
a man – pen and paper are my tools, I can't lay a path
or chop a tree or tend a horse and if someone said fight
then –

**Delio** what's got into you?

**Antonio** I'm in love

**Delio** oh right

**Antonio** and it's terrible. Go on – ask me about it

**Delio** well, with who?

*Antonio looks around. He whispers in his friend's ear.*

*Delio looks incredulous.*

**Antonio** exactly

**Delio** how long has this been going on?

**Antonio** keep your voice down . . . we were married in
her bedchamber, I call her Giovanna –

**Delio** how can I keep my voice down –?

**Antonio** seriously, you mustn't tell anyone, it's a secret

45

**Delio** alright, but why the despair?

**Antonio** because I am not her equal and I wish I were. Think about it, why would someone like the Duchess choose me? I mean really? She wouldn't. There is no reason why she would. Surely she will soon realise her mistake. There is not a single thing about me that is remarkable, nothing that she couldn't find in other men, and in better men

tell me, do you see anything that especially commends me?

**Delio** I see plenty of things

**Antonio** what do you mean? I'm weak –

**Delio** you don't even know what you are, that's the thing about you

**Antonio** that isn't even a thing, can you build a wall with that?

**Delio** do you want to build a wall?

**Antonio** I want to be a man, if that is what it takes then I'll build a wall

**Delio** you have no idea how lovely you are.

**Antonio** don't try and cheer me up

**Delio** what does it matter if you are already married?

**Antonio** I want her to love me as I love her
I want her to respect me as I respect her

**Delio** does she say she does?

**Antonio** yes, but that is just words.
anyone could say that, and not mean it at all. How can we trust what another thinks of us?

**Delio** you can trust actions, does she seem to love you?

**Antonio** I suppose

**Delio** and in bed?

**Antonio** yes, in bed yes

**Delio** then my dear friend, maybe she does love you

**Antonio** I should grow a beard do you think. And try to breed some muscles. I could exercise my thighs so they were thick and round

**Delio** I think you will still be you.

**Antonio** Then I am doomed. I never thought I would find a woman. But now I have one, I find I am in greater torment.

**Delio** does it not mean anything if I were to say I think you are excellent? Fine as you are, and the most wonderful of men.

**Antonio** yes my friend, it means fuck all.


### SEVEN: DELIO

*Delio and Julia. In bed. Together but apart.*

**Delio** people are so inconstant, don't you think?
    you think them to be one thing and then suddenly they
are another.

**Julia** I don't know what you are talking about –

**Delio** how can someone change so quickly
    or maybe they were always as they are –
    and what can you ever know really?
    what can you believe –

**Julia** can't we just go to sleep?

**Delio** take us
    we say we love each other every night
    but do either of us believe a single word?

47

**Julia**  I'm really tired –

**Delio**  we are a poor fit in the end.
   we know it
   you married me because you thought I would have
money
   I married you because I liked your smile
   turns out i have no money
   and you hardly ever smile

**Julia**  goodnight.

**Delio**  you could be loving another, so could I.
   we sleep beside each other, is that enough? When I am
here at least and that is hardly ever

**Julia**  is that enough?

**Delio**  yes, is that enough?

**Julia**  is that enough for you?

*Beat.*

**Delio**  I don't know, that is all I am saying.
   sometimes I think we are strangers.
   I wouldn't blame you if you loved another.

**Julia**  you wouldn't blame me?

**Delio**  no.
   would you blame me?

**Julia**  I don't know

**Delio**  what the hell actually is it, this thing called love?
   it isn't something that happens between us, is it?
   would we ever dare tell each other that we loved the
wrong people?

## EIGHT: JULIA

*Julia is sitting, waking up in bed. Awake now. Wondering about what Delio had said.*

*She looks at the Cardinal's ring on her finger.*

*Antonio takes the microphone and sings a song about love.*

*Ferdinand sings too. Crazy fucked-up love.*

*Julia joins in. What we will do for it and how it kills us in the end.*

## Act Two

*Bosola and Antonio are kicking a football back and forth.*

**Bosola**  how can you call me melancholic?

**Antonio**  I only said –

**Bosola**  a little philosophic?

**Antonio**  a little given to long contemplation of a philosophic nature, yes

**Bosola**  contemplation is the means to a remedy

**Antonio**  pass the ball

**Bosola**  okay, here's another
our widowed duchess
is sick a lot, have you noticed?

**Antonio**  no

**Bosola**  really? She pukes, her stomach seethes
her eyelids are almost blue

**Antonio**  can't say I have looked

**Bosola**  she's lost weight on the face, and grown fat on the thigh –

**Antonio**  oh –

**Bosola**  yes and – unlike current fashion – she is wearing these floaty things

*Bosola picks up the football and looks at Antonio.*

**Antonio**  perhaps they're more comfortable

**Bosola**  but why? She is a beautiful woman who now dresses in tents

**Antonio**  well, I don't know

**Bosola**  she's been at it

**Antonio**  what?

**Bosola**  yes, with someone and you know what comes then –

**Antonio**  that's stupid, no –

*Beat.*

**Bosola**  it's okay, I've got this trick

**Antonio**  what trick?

**Bosola**  well, if it's as we think –

**Antonio**  we don't think

**Bosola**  I'll offer her something, and
     you watch
     many a promiscuous woman is exposed this way

**Antonio**  what do you mean?

**Bosola**  apricots. Irresistible to those with a . . . you know . . . in the oven

**Antonio**  isn't that an old wives' tale?

**Bosola**  I think she might be an old wife. My point exactly

**Antonio**  we all like apricots

**Bosola**  there's like and like, you watch

*The Duchess comes in attended by Cariola.*

**Duchess**  your arm, Cariola

**Cariola**  I'm here

**Antonio**  but what if we –

**Bosola**  oh stop, it's nothing

**Duchess**  I feel so fat –

**Cariola**  fat? You look fine to me

**Bosola**  she does look a little fat to me, now you mention it

**Antonio**  thin. I would say

**Duchess**  I am exceedingly short-winded today
   Bosola, I would have you get a chair that is a little
lower, it will help my back

**Bosola**  didn't the Duchess of Florence have one like it?

**Duchess**  did she?

**Bosola**  which she used when she was great with child

**Antonio**  I bet she used it at other times as well

**Duchess**  no, I think he's right, she did do that

*Cariola comes to help her.*

urgg, your hair smells of lemon pills, what have you
done?

**Bosola**  you see, now she complains of the smell –

**Duchess**  ahh, I'm going to puke right here it's so strong

**Antonio**  madam, calm yourself

**Duchess**  I am calm
   who said I wasn't calm? I am CALM. Calm calm.

**Bosola**  you see, her mood swings up and down

**Antonio**  my lady, perhaps you need to sit down

**Duchess**  yes, I need to sit, didn't I just say that
   no don't touch me
   did I say you could touch?

bring me some water – would you, dear?
no, not water
some milk
no, not milk either
some duck
no, not duck
chicken
no
pork
no
bread no, cheese no

**Bosola**  madam, would you like some apricots?

**Duchess**  apricots?

**Bosola**  yes

**Antonio**  apricots are out of season

**Duchess**  apricots, that's what I want, get me apricots

**Antonio**  you can't get apricots in April, he was only –

**Bosola**  I have some here

**Duchess**  well look at that, he has the very thing I fancy

**Antonio**  but maybe what you fancy is not what in fact you need

**Bosola**  but why not? I think the Duchess of Florence liked these too

**Duchess**  where did you get them?

**Antonio**  don't eat them, madam

**Duchess**  oh shush

**Bosola**  ahh, I spent a lot on them, a young gardener ripened them early

**Antonio**  that means in horse dung, yuk

**Bosola** would you like to taste one?

**Antonio** they smell of shit, better not

**Duchess** they smell divine

**Antonio** early fruit is bad for the stomach

**Duchess** can something so irresistible be so bad?

**Bosola** here, I'll eat one, show they are quite pleasant

*He starts to eat.*

see, good in fact

*The Duchess is salivating.*

**Antonio** I'll get you some another day
come on, let's go back inside

**Bosola** would you like to try?

*The Duchess grabs them off Bosola.*

*She eats them greedily, like a savage.*

**Duchess** good, they are good
they are mmmm, in fact they are –

**Antonio** please, madam

**Duchess** mmmm mmmm

*She looks at Antonio and greedily eats more.*

*Almost orgasmic.*

**Duchess** mmmmm mmmmm mmmm oh mmmm

**Bosola** she seems to enjoy them anyway

**Duchess** the horseman knew what I needed oh wow
oh wow oh wow

**Antonio** you have juice down your chin

*She wipes.*

*She burps.*

**Duchess**  any more?

*Bosola looks into his bag.*

**Bosola**  alas, only one

**Duchess**  give it

**Bosola**  are you sure you want it?

**Duchess**  I'm sure –

**Bosola**  hang on –

*He toys with her.*

*She grabs the last apricot.*

*Eats it fast.*

**Duchess**  ahhh, mmmm, ooooo that was –

*They watch her lick her lips.*

who knew that they were so delicious?

*Bosola looks at Antonio.*

**Bosola**  so we can take it, she likes them

**Duchess**  get more, will you?
more more more
I need apricots.
apricots

**Bosola**  I will I will, now I know you like apricots

**Antonio**  everyone likes apricots

**Bosola**  not everyone likes them like that

*She burps again.*

**Duchess**  oh dear

**Cariola**  what, madam?

**Duchess**  well, just then, after
it's alright I just think I need to –

*She burps again.*

and perhaps a –

*She tries to fart.*

oh no, hang on
  oh actually I don't feel well and this swelling, they sit
hard in my stomach

*Bosola is laughing.*

**Bosola**  can she swell more?

**Antonio**  what have you done to her?

**Bosola**  she has done this to herself, I told you we would
find her out
  mark my words, there is a child in there

**Duchess**  I need to go to my room. Oh dear, I think this is
  oh, there is pain now

**Bosola**  all women are the same
  they can't resist us men

**Cariola**  madam, take my arm

**Bosola**  the act, it's like they have no control

**Antonio**  it might just be wind
  it's wind, isn't it?

**Duchess**  this isn't wind

*She leaves.*

**Bosola**  I have to say I am surprised by the Duchess
though –

**Cariola**  lock the gates, tell the servants no one may come
or leave
  and get yourself back to the stables

**Bosola**  let me stay a while, I am worried for the lady

**Cariola**  this is orders from the lady

**Bosola**  I didn't hear her say it

**Cariola**  steward, tell the horseman to leave this room

**Antonio**  but

**Cariola**  who is greater in this room, you or him?

**Antonio**  . . . ?

**Bosola**  I'm going.

*Beat.*

*Bosola leaves.*

*Antonio and Cariola are left.*

**Cariola**  good grief

**Antonio**  is it labour?

**Cariola**  yes

**Antonio**  I mean is this actually labour?

**Cariola**  yes

**Antonio**  you mean that labour has started?

**Cariola**  stop asking the same question. This is labour, yes

**Antonio**  a baby will come?

**Cariola**  yes, fuck's sake, yes, that is the normal course of events IN LABOUR

**Antonio**  what if I faint?

**Cariola**  If you faint I will roll you out of the door and leave you for the pigeons
    but really I think it is the Duchess that we be thinking about
    it's weeks early, and if she has the baby here, then everyone will know

**Antonio** can't we get her away?

**Cariola** I have no idea how much time we have.

**Antonio** you have no idea?

**Cariola** no, I have no idea

*The Duchess moans.*

**Antonio** you have to sort this

**Cariola** the baby is coming, what more is there to sort?

*The Duchess groans.*

roll up your sleeves, I'll talk you through it.

**Antonio** what?


*The Cardinal is in his office.*

*Julia comes in.*

**Cardinal** oh.

**Julia** you sound surprised

**Cardinal** well, yes, a little perhaps. I thought, since I hadn't seen you –

**Julia** my husband is away

**Cardinal** again?

**Julia** all month.
  maybe longer.

**Cardinal** how lovely.

**Julia** he has left me all alone.

*Beat.*

*He finishes what is he doing.*

**Julia** I thought you might be –

**Cardinal** what?

**Julia** interested?

**Cardinal** yes, I am

**Julia** I have been thinking of you a lot of the time.

*He looks at her.*

*She looks at him.*

**Cardinal** I am just about to say mass.

*He goes back to his work.*

*She stands there, not sure.*

**Julia** shall I wait then?

**Cardinal** I will be with you when I am ready.

**Julia** only –

**Cardinal** what, after keeping me waiting for months, you mind waiting for a minute or two?

**Julia** I thought you'd be pleased.

**Cardinal** I am pleased. Only do I wonder if there is some other reason that you have arrived at my door? I heard your husband is bankrupt

**Julia** I'm not asking for anything

**Cardinal** take your top off

**Julia** I'm not here for money

**Cardinal** oh, I don't care, I'll give you money take your top off, take your top off

**Julia** what?

**Cardinal** well, if we are to have intercourse

**Julia** okay, but do you have to say it like –

**Cardinal** I thought that was what you came for?

**Julia** but like this?

**Cardinal** take off your top.

**Julia** and if I say no?

**Cardinal** you don't get to say no.
    you're my mistress now. You're either desperate or you love me, both put you at a disadvantage. Smile smile. I'm joking. Here, hang on, let me just finish the sacrament.
    take off your top and remove your underclothes
    I'll just drink the wine

**Julia** must you say it so?

**Cardinal** I really don't see, you are here to lie with me aren't you? That is why you came. So you need to remove some of your clothing.

*He grabs her.*

if you love me then you will do what I ask without question.
    say you love me

*He tries to kiss her.*

**Julia** I did say that

**Cardinal** say it again

**Julia** I love you

**Cardinal** say I love you more than him

**Julia** I love you more than him

**Cardinal** say he is stupid and ugly and has lost all his money

**Julia** he is stupid and ugly and has lost all his money

**Cardinal** say his dick is tiny

**Julia**  his dick is tiny

**Cardinal**  that's it, now take your top off

*She takes her top off.*

very good
  now turn around.
  lift your skirt and touch yourself, and repeat what you
said

**Julia**  please –

**Cardinal**  what?

**Julia**  can you not make me feel so –

**Cardinal**  what? Sordid
  you want to be my mistress
  you are coming here when you are married to another
  what has the church got to say about that?

*He grabs her, starts to have sex with her on the floor.*

**Julia**  don't hurt me

**Cardinal**  what, like you have hurt me all these months?
  it's alright, it will pass. I won't hurt you much, gentle
gentle oh yes
  that's it, fight sweetheart, that only makes it more, yes
see you like it now, I'll look after you, you can have what
you want

**Ferdinand**  knock knock

**Cardinal**  Christ, brother, a little warning

**Ferdinand**  you gave me a key
  very sorry.

*Julia and the Cardinal get themselves together.*

*She looks at him.*

**Cardinal**  shush, shush you'll come back

**Julia**  what if I don't?

**Cardinal**  then you won't. But with so few options I suspect you will.

*Julia leaves.*

*Ferdinand sits down on the Cardinal's desk.*

*The Cardinal is still doing his zip up.*

**Ferdinand**  for God's sake. I've seen it before

**Cardinal**  why are you here?

**Ferdinand**  proof. It's a sort of poison, isn't it, to finally know?

**Cardinal**  what are you talking about?

**Ferdinand**  she she she she she she she

**Cardinal**  who who who who who?

**Ferdinand**  she's had a baby

**Cardinal**  what?

**Ferdinand**  that's what I heard

**Cardinal**  how?

**Ferdinand**  you mean, dear brother, you don't know how we make babies?

**Cardinal**  keep your voice down

**Ferdinand**  no point keeping it quiet now
    it's going to be shouted around the town. The widowed duchess has produced a child. Shout it. A baby a baby a baby a baby a baby a baby

**Cardinal**  can you be angry without this rupture?

**Ferdinand**  rupture? Not from me. I am quite composed.

*The Cardinal takes a piece of paper.*

should we kill her?
    she is clearly trying to kill us in reputation
    what do you suggest, murder?

**Cardinal** let me read this

**Ferdinand** she is a whore. So death is probably the only way out –

**Cardinal** you aren't even letting me think –

**Ferdinand** but thought is exactly what I am proposing, an exploration of the problem, a tossing of ideas forward and back. A conference between us. Maybe we should have their bodies, hers and the lover, burnt in coal pit? Hmm? and the air-hole blocked so their evil smoke might not go up to heaven, or! kill them both by burning their skin with sulphur and then light a match? Or boil the bastard brats in a pot perhaps and make a stew to serve up to the lecherous father

**Cardinal** sit down would you

**Ferdinand** WHAT IS THE CHURCH GOING TO SAY?

*The Cardinal sits down, reads.*

your own sister –

**Cardinal** I don't know

**Ferdinand** and we can't hush it up. Not with a baby
    perhaps we toss her palace about her ears then, yes, that first
    root up her all her land, sell all her property and dump her out on the street as waste –
    wait – can you hear laughing?

**Cardinal** no . . . ?

**Ferdinand** yes, there –
    listen harder, they are already laughing at us, excellent hyenas

even in the corridor the word is out, or perhaps it is
her, her laughter carried by the air
    no, it's not a woman, it's a man. It's her lover.

**Cardinal**  are you stark mad?

**Ferdinand**  some strong barge-man with thighs like tree
trunks,
    yes, he's laughing while he fucks her
    or one of the woodyard that is sporty and can throw
a hammer perhaps, or maybe some lovely squire that
carries coals up to her lodgings and recites poetry

**Cardinal**  you seem to go beyond reason

**Ferdinand**  stop it, mistress, stop

**Cardinal**  what has happened to you?

**Ferdinand**  I don't know, there's something in my eye

**Cardinal**  there is nothing in your eye

**Ferdinand**  I don't want to see, I don't want to hear

**Cardinal**  come on, pull yourself together

**Ferdinand**  I see her all around. Hear her. Groaning
squealing.
    undressed and with men
    can't you see too?

**Cardinal**  you are thinking too much, calm down. This is
all anger, nothing else

**Ferdinand**  something must be wrong with our family
that heaven is taking revenge

**Cardinal**  there is nothing wrong with us

**Ferdinand**  oh, there she is again, grunting now.
    no wonder I don't sleep. I haven't slept well for a long
time. How could anyone sleep when she is making such
a racket?

**Cardinal** you aren't well

**Ferdinand** I am perfectly fine. A little tired
a lullaby does it

**Cardinal** a lullaby?

**Ferdinand** yes, one that was sung to us
anything that blocks it out –

*Ferdinand sings it.*

you know it? Sing sing.

*Cardinal looks at him, worried.*


*Antonio and the Duchess.*

*The Duchess is breast-feeding one of the twins. She sings
a lullaby.*

**Duchess** look at the little face

**Antonio** there there

**Duchess** he's sucking his lip, how is the other one?

**Cariola** sleeping finally

**Duchess** I need to feed her too

**Cariola** they should be having a bottle
both is too much for one person

**Duchess** and miss this?

*They look at the baby.*

**Antonio** to produce one was a miracle but twins

**Duchess** runs in the family, you were warned

**Antonio** I love it, I want more
next time triplets, quins
we'll have an army

*Cariola goes to the shutters.*

**Duchess**  no, leave the shutters open, these children are
born in hiding, they can have some air at night

**Cariola**  let me take him now, you need some sleep –

**Duchess**  yes, bring me my nightdress, and a brush
let me say goodnight to the girl
you'll have to sleep somewhere else as well

**Antonio**  really?

**Duchess**  sorry

**Antonio**  I can't persuade you?
even if I go down on to my knees to ask for a night's
lodgings –

**Duchess**  I am pretty tired

**Antonio**  don't send me away, I have work to do

**Duchess**  you'll keep me awake

**Antonio**  yes, that's the point, I'll keep you awake
alright, we'll sleep, we'll sleep, that's all
if I can wrap my arms around you

**Duchess**  ah, but if we sleep, where is the fun in that?

**Antonio**  you read my mind

**Duchess**  but they will be up in three hours

**Antonio**  oh, poor you, torn by pleasure

**Cariola**  my lord I have shared a bed with her often and
I know
it's her that will keep you up

**Antonio**  oh really?

**Duchess**  oi

**Cariola**  she's sprawls across the bed

**Antonio**  what is wrong with sprawling?

66

**Cariola**  and she snores

**Duchess**  I do not

**Antonio**  actually you do a bit

**Cariola**  sir, can I ask you a question?

**Antonio**  go on, Cariola

**Cariola**  well, when you spend the night here, why do you get up so early?

**Duchess**  yes, why do you do that?

**Antonio**  ah that's easy, by the morning –

**Cariola**  he's had enough

**Antonio**  not nearly but actually I can take no more –

**Duchess**  oh stop it –

**Antonio**  she's rampant

*She kisses him.*

ah, but that's one. I need two to see me through the night. give me another.

*She kisses him again.*

maybe you do love me?

**Duchess**  finally, you've worked it out!

**Antonio**  I still don't understand why –

**Cariola**  good question

**Duchess**  then let it be a mystery

**Cariola**  really, sir, we must leave her.
the babies will be up before long and looking for milk

**Duchess**  goodnight both.

*She kisses Antonio.*

*He starts to go.*

*He comes back in and kisses her again.*

**Antonio** if you change your mind –

**Duchess** save that thought.
   but let me sleep.

*He goes.*

*She picks up the babies.*

shush shush, don't wake up. I only wanted to look at
you. To tell you, that apart from your brother, you are
the most beautiful thing that ever lived. Both of you.
Made of alabaster and carved by a master craftsman.
Shush shush, don't cry. But then even your crying is the
most perfect sound –

*Ferdinand appears behind her.*

*She sees him in the mirror.*

*Beat.*

*She puts the twins down.*

**Ferdinand** congratulations

**Duchess** thank you, Ferdinand

**Ferdinand** let's not be hasty. Ferdinand? Tut tut
   you know my name but I don't know yours

**Duchess** what?

**Ferdinand** I don't know how to say your name, because
we haven't met

**Duchess** I'm your sister

**Ferdinand** my sister no, she is a widow

**Duchess** she got married

**Ferdinand** married? Not her –

**Duchess**  yes, I am married

*Ferdinand comes and picks up the baby.*

**Ferdinand**  a second congratulations then if you are she.
  A married woman *and* with a baby

**Duchess**  thank you

**Ferdinand**  harlot.

*Beat.*

*The Duchess doesn't know how to read him.*

but hang on, there's one and another – two?

**Duchess**  yes, twins

**Ferdinand**  no

*He looks confused for a second.*

twins, really, sister?

**Duchess**  yes

**Ferdinand**  twins? Twins twins twins twins twins?

**Duchess**  yes sir.

**Ferdinand**  is one a boy and one a girl?

**Duchess**  yes, exactly

**Ferdinand**  like us?

**Duchess**  like us

**Ferdinand**  which one is this?

*She looks.*

**Duchess**  that's the boy

**Ferdinand**  the boy. Congratulations on your boy

**Duchess**  Nico

**Ferdinand**  that's my middle name.
　　sweet Nico, Nico
　　what am I thinking, Nico
　　someone poked your mother and that made you
　　this wasn't a marriage

**Duchess**  it was a marriage

**Ferdinand**  married, married, sorry I keep forgetting.
Married married. Congratulations
　　but a secret wedding, what a pity. You want to get
married you get married in a church not in a bedroom,
I wanted to wear a hat

**Duchess**  well, I realise that you –

**Ferdinand**  someone poked your mother, boy
　　someone poked your mother, how though I am
wondering
　　from behind or up the arse

**Duchess**  stop

**Ferdinand**  you don't want your son to hear it? Nico
　　your mother would rather I didn't talk about your
daddy, and his towering erection, so let's not mention it.
You were found under a cloud. A bush, no penis made
you

**Duchess**  men and women get married all the time

**Ferdinand**  poke, you mean
　　they poke all the time

**Duchess**  men and women get married, I don't see why
mine is so offensive

**Ferdinand**  offensive?
　　offensive, if it was just offensive I might simply be
offended. But this is not a marriage, this is carnal desire
　　with a bedroom contract to cover yourselves

**Duchess**  you're breaking my heart

**Ferdinand**  your heart! Your heart
  I am sorry, my darling, how could I break your heart?
You're married you're married. It's just a thing to get
used to.

*He coos with the baby.*

oh, but let me hold the girl

*He puts the boy twin down too roughly, the Duchess
catches him.*

*Ferdinand goes to the other twin.*

this the girl?

**Duchess**  yes

**Ferdinand**  not as pretty as you

**Duchess**  she isn't yet a month

**Ferdinand**  no hair
  double chins

**Duchess**  her name is Isabella

**Ferdinand**  Isabella
  is a bell a necessary on an Isabella
  no Isabella let me sing you this

*He sings the lullaby again, a slightly fucked-up version.*

**Duchess**  can you be rational for a second, I know you
are angry but –

**Ferdinand**  angry? No, how could I be angry
  you smell different

*He puts the baby down.*

**Duchess**  I smell of milk

**Ferdinand**  disgusting

**Duchess**  you used to love me

**Ferdinand**  I do love you
    of course I love you.

*He sniffs again.*

**Ferdinand**  it's not milk, it's vinegar

**Duchess**  no –

**Ferdinand**  you have curdled

*He sniffs around.*

why can't I even sniff you now? we were together in the
womb, weren't we, two babies. I know your smell.
Imagine we were intertwined, then, limb around limb –
    you said you loved me

**Duchess**  I do

**Ferdinand**  well here let me get accustomed to this new
aroma

**Duchess**  get off

**Ferdinand**  see this
    this is our father's knife.
    if I thought it was you that was rotten I would use it.
    I would cut out whatever part of you had turned
putrid.

**Duchess**  that isn't our father's knife

**Ferdinand**  it is, and I would hate to see it grow rusty.

**Duchess**  you don't scare me

**Ferdinand**  no scare, no no no. I only mean to restore
you.

*He pushes her down.*

*He grapples with her on the floor.*

he is the one that we must find and cut out.

*He sings to her a lullaby from childhood, he rocks her.*

*He tries to cuddle in to her.*

**Duchess**  you aren't yourself

*He throws everything in the air.*

**Ferdinand**  it's just my eyes, they –

**Duchess**  what has happened to you?

**Ferdinand**  nothing.

*He pushes her away.*

nothing.
   it's you, you make me like this.
   it's you it's you it's you

*Ferdinand leaves.*

*The Duchess is left with the babies.*

*Cariola and Antonio come back in.*

*Silence and shock.*

**Duchess**  I don't know what to make of him –

**Antonio**  he must have had a key

**Cariola**  the side door isn't locked –

**Duchess**  it's like he has lost himself

**Antonio**  I shouldn't have left you alone; I should have defended you

**Duchess**  it's better that you didn't

**Cariola**  I heard he doesn't sleep any more

**Duchess**  more than lack of sleep has made this.

*She puts his knife down.*

you have to get away. None of us can stay here. But you especially

pack a bag, go
why is no one moving? Go!

*A knock is heard.*

*Beat.*

you'll have to go quickly.
    I know its not fair and we shouldn't have to hide.

**Antonio** leave the palace?

**Duchess** it hasn't occurred to my brother that I would
marry my servant, but when he finds you –

*A second knock.*

*Antonio goes.*

yes? Who is it?

**Bosola** Bosola, madam.

*Duchess looks at Cariola.*

**Duchess** hide the children

**Cariola** where?

*The Duchess shows her behind a curtain.*

*Bosola comes in.*

**Bosola** your brother says to tell you he will be back with
the Cardinal

**Duchess** tonight?

**Bosola** he told me to let no one sleep. I have to say he
looked even wilder than usual

**Duchess** Antonio, my steward, and master of our
household
    has tricked me, all of us
    and tried to swindle me out of money

**Bosola** Antonio?

**Duchess** yes, you know I have always trusted him, well
  my brother and I had borrowed some money and
  and Antonio it seems has syphoned some away

**Bosola** strange

**Duchess** I know, that is what I thought because he is a
good steward I always thought he was honest

**Bosola** yes

**Duchess** but here we find
  my brother's bills at Naples are held against funds
here –
  and neither can be paid

**Bosola** are you sure?

**Duchess** my brother just gave me the evidence
  we can't prove it of course but –
  who else has access to my accounts but Antonio?
  call up our officers

**Bosola** now?

**Duchess** yes, I need to dismiss him and send him away

**Bosola** this evening?

**Duchess** yes, right now, I need to show my brothers that
I can restore order. Or do you think I need to wait for the
men, to handle this? I am the one that has been conned,
so let me rip out the rascal.

*Bosola exits.*

*Duchess alone for a second.*

**Duchess** oh good grief good grief.

*Antonio comes back.*

*And Cariola brings the babies.*

you have got everything you need?
  where can you go?

**Antonio** Delio is in Ancona this month

**Duchess** I'll send some money and jewels. Our safety is precarious, we mustn't say much more. I'm going to accuse you of theft, it's all I can do

**Antonio** theft?

**Duchess** fraud then, both

**Antonio** but

**Duchess** the officers are on their way. We don't have time to argue. Take the twins, get them away too.

**Antonio** the twins?

**Duchess** yes, the twins have to go with you

**Antonio** I can't take them

**Duchess** you have to. Cariola, get their stuff ready – and wait for him by the back door

**Antonio** can you be parted from them?

**Duchess** no, never. I can't imagine it but it is better than seeing them harmed. Here, let me say goodbye, oh no, it's worse to say goodbye

**Antonio** I can't do this

**Duchess** you have to, here, this is or you, and this for our son and this for our –
  let me kiss you once more for that look came from a dying father, best of my life, don't say it. Best of your life is ahead. Go. Take them to Cariola. I have to accuse you publicly
  no wait, not both. Take the boy but leave me the girl. no, take the girl and leave the boy, no, how can I chose?

**Antonio** we will all be back together before long

**Duchess** promise me that, and you must keep your word

*They kiss again.*

*He gives her a twin.*

which is this?

**Antonio** Isabella

**Duchess** Isabella I will keep then. Take Nico with you. Cariola, are you there?

**Cariola** yes

**Duchess** get Nico to the back door with this stuff

*She hands both to Cariola.*

*Duchess turns to Antonio.*

**Duchess** are you ready for this?
  get down on your knees
  wait

*She kisses him.*

*Then she hits him.*

**Antonio** ow

**Duchess** did that hurt?

**Antonio** yes

**Duchess** good

*Then hits him again.*

**Antonio** don't do it like this

**Duchess** I have to do it.

*Re-enter Bosola and officers.*

**Antonio** I beg you to reconsider –

**Duchess** gentlemen

let this man be an example to you all

**Antonio**  Duchess –

**Duchess**  he broke my trust and for that I am dismissing him. No payment, no reference, no handshake or goodbye.

**Antonio**  now that isn't fair

**Duchess**  this isn't a trial, you don't get to speak

**Antonio**  not even to defend myself?

**Duchess**  not even that
    I am confiscating everything you have
    you will leave immediately

**Antonio**  I just think the way you are –

**Duchess**  so, sir, you have your pass to leave
    I am not sure what keeps you here

**Antonio**  you may see, gentlemen, she makes decisions hastily

**Duchess**  take him away

**Antonio**  is that it? Is that all the defence I get?

**Duchess**  yes, that is it.
    piss off.

*Antonio is taken off.*

*The Duchess and Bosola watch him go.*

**Bosola**  are you sure you acted wisely?

**Duchess**  what do the staff think of him?

**Bosola**  they like him, I think

**Duchess**  really? They don't like anyone

**Bosola**  alright, they think he uses too much of the soap on his clothes

**Duchess**  oh?

**Bosola**  smells a little too much of perfume

**Duchess**  aha?

**Bosola**  yes, and sits a little too much in front of the fire

**Duchess**  right

**Bosola**  some say in fact he is a hermaphrodite

**Duchess**  I've heard enough.

**Bosola**  you didn't ask me what I think
I think Antonio is utterly straightforward. Honest.
if there was a mix-up with funds, then there'll be
an explanation

**Duchess**  you think that?

**Bosola**  yes, the man no more would have robbed you
than robbed his own mother.

**Duchess**  I'm glad you think that.

**Bosola**  you just banished him –

**Duchess**  oh yes, that.
so I did.
Antonio is my husband, we are married

**Bosola**  what?

**Duchess**  in secret, but it's binding, we did it here

**Bosola**  here?

**Duchess**  yes in this room

**Bosola**  you married your servant?

**Duchess**  I liked him

*Bosola laughs.*

**Bosola**  you married a man because you liked him?

**Duchess**  what's wrong with that?

**Bosola**  I didn't think your class ever did that –

**Duchess**  I have had two babies by him

**Bosola**  good grief

**Duchess**  I shouldn't have told you. I'm not thinking

**Bosola**  I'll wear it on the inside of my heart

**Duchess**  I am going to give you some money now, and some jewels
  I want you to follow him to Ancona

**Bosola**  why so far?

**Duchess**  we have to get him right away from here, my brothers know about the babies and are raging.
  in a few days I am going to follow him
  will you help me?

**Bosola**  here is my first thought, don't just disappear

**Duchess**  no?

**Bosola**  it will look odd
  pretend you are going on a pilgrimage

**Duchess**  a pilgrimage?

**Bosola**  no one will question that.

**Duchess**  I've never been on a pilgrimage

**Bosola**  there is Our Lady of Loreto, very near Ancona, say you are going there

**Duchess**  to do what?

**Bosola**  pray

**Duchess**  oh

**Bosola**  arouse less suspicion

**Duchess** good thinking
  Cariola

*Cariola appears.*

did you hear that? can you start to get ready for our
journey

**Cariola** can I say something?

**Duchess** of course, go ahead

**Cariola** this pilgrimage idea, I just think –

**Bosola** what?

**Cariola** I don't like this poking around with religion
  feigning something, it feels a bit –

**Duchess** a bit?

**Cariola** sacrilegious

**Bosola** sacrilegious?

**Cariola** some of us actually believe in God

**Bosola** you are a superstitious fool then

**Cariola** I prefer to believe in God than the devil

**Bosola** lucky you

**Duchess** I tell you what, if we see a shrine on the way
I will say a quick prayer
  thank you, Bosola, for your advice, I'm going to take it.
  I haven't been on a pilgrimage, and maybe I should.

*She goes off.*

**Cariola** that was bad advice

**Bosola** she needs a proper reason, she can't just go

**Cariola** you never think things through

**Bosola** don't I?

**Cariola** I have been watching you for months

you are rushed and sloppy.

**Bosola**  I thought I thought things too much?

**Cariola**  you think like a man, from the outside

**Bosola**  well, you think like a woman, changing one's mind, and if the Duchess suddenly declares she is going on a pilgrimage, everyone will think how out of character and like a woman

**Cariola**  do you ever have a good word to say for women?

**Bosola**  I know where I am with men

**Cariola**  was there never a woman you liked?

**Bosola**  no.
    my mother?

*Cariola goes right up to him.*

**Cariola**  not even her.

**Bosola**  why did you say that?

**Cariola**  because all light is gone from you

*He pulls her back.*

*He kisses her roughly, she kisses him too.*

**Bosola**  you know I am working for her brother.

**Cariola**  I suspected
    a spy?

**Bosola**  I'm telling you the truth now

**Cariola**  too late.

*He kisses her again.*

**Bosola**  what is it you want?

**Cariola**  if there is a good man in there, give us a little while.

don't tell them anything until she is gone.

and say she went to Germany for her pilgrimage, send them the wrong way –

**Bosola**  you're trying to pull me in two

**Cariola**  that's the devil then pulling at you. Make the right choice.

*She kisses him. More tender now.*

I almost wonder if we could have been something you and me.

*Cariola leaves.*

*Bosola is alone.*

**Bosola**  I am like the devil's quilted anvil, the blows are never heard.

I have to tell my master? That's it. My job. For if I say she has gone to Germany and lie to him, then what am I? Nah. I have a code. I do what the master asks for. This is just some devilish torment, and the base quality of the spy perhaps. She shouldn't have kissed me. I have a code.

God, I can feel you now.

loyalty is my arrow, it's the only code I know.

*Behind him the walls start to drip with blood.*

*Interval.*

# Act Three

*The Duchess is in a makeshift cell. There is nothing in it except a chair.*

*Ferdinand is outside and observing her.*

*The Cardinal comes in to speak to Ferdinand.*

**Cardinal**  how is she?

**Ferdinand**  as you would expect –

**Cardinal**  still sick?

**Ferdinand**  not sick

**Cardinal**  sick of the soul, the soul, you said she was sick of the soul

**Ferdinand**  she is sick of the soul

**Cardinal**  that is why she is here in this hospital you have made for her.

**Ferdinand**  yes yes, sick of the soul, yes

*Beat.*

**Cardinal**  because if she isn't sick, we have just –

**Ferdinand**  she is sick

*They look at her in the prison they have made.*

tell me how to resolve it quicker?

**Cardinal**  I don't know but four years –

**Ferdinand**  what do you suggest – she cannot go if she is not cured? For then we have achieved nothing. And that is worse. What will she say about this?

**Cardinal**  put the light on

*He looks through the glass at the Duchess.*

good grief

*Beat.*

**Ferdinand**  go back to your mass, and forget it, I will solve her. She must be near to her breaking point now

**Cardinal**  surely. You need to sort this.

*Bosola goes in to see the Duchess.*

**Bosola**  all comfort to you

**Duchess**  comfort?

**Bosola**  I just meant –

**Duchess**  what, this my comfort? A chair. Not even a window. A trough of water to wash myself and my life dripping by.

**Bosola**  your brother is outside

**Duchess**  to do what?

**Bosola**  to speak with you.

**Duchess**  oh, he wants to talk now?

**Bosola**  he asked me to put the lights on low so he doesn't have to look at you

**Duchess**  because I am disgusting?

**Bosola**  I am just telling you what he said –

*The lights dim.*

**Duchess**  okay. Okay. Here I am. Disgusting me.
    are you in the room? Are you a shadow?

I must still smell, even more since I have been here.

**Ferdinand** so soon we get to your grievance?

**Duchess** you can't keep me prisoner for ever

**Ferdinand** madam, this is a place of healing, I told you, we hope to cure your mania

**Duchess** someone will find out, I must have been missed

**Ferdinand** your pilgrimage idea was a good one, everyone thinks you went away and stayed there.

**Duchess** for all these years?

**Ferdinand** anyway, you aren't held captive. You're your own guest, have you never been to your own basement?

**Duchess** what?

*The Duchess looks around.*

**Ferdinand** we made a few adjustments but you are your own host

**Duchess** oh hell

**Ferdinand** I see we have much work to do. How can you call hell like that?

**Duchess** even in this dark room several floors beneath my own palace, I can call hell.

**Ferdinand** we don't blame you, we think you are faultless. Just so you know.
    your sex was the source of evil, Satan brought you to your crime

**Duchess** what crime?

**Ferdinand** adultery, what crime?!

**Duchess** we were married, I LOVED HIM

**Ferdinand**  tcch, that word. I see you are still confused

**Duchess**  let me see you
   I want to see if there is any trace of you left

**Ferdinand**  will I give you my hand? let you kiss it

**Duchess**  I would rather gnaw at it than kiss it.

**Ferdinand**  here. Bite it then.

**Duchess**  put the lights on, let me see your face

**Ferdinand**  you want the lights?

**Duchess**  yes, I want the lights, what is going on?

*The lights come on.*


*Ferdinand has gone.*

*A bit of video comes on to the screen behind her. The film is of Antonio and Nico, now aged three or four, standing against a wall.*

**Duchess**  Antonio – and there Nico. Nico, darling –

*Suddenly we see them being shot with bullets and falling down dead.*

oh God
   oh God, no?

*Ferdinand talks to her through the speaker system in the cell. He drops down a microphone.*

**Ferdinand**  you've come to your senses. There is no point holding out for him.
   whether you loved him or not, it's just us now.

*She doesn't answer. Sits on her chair.*

*The image goes.*

I said, have you had enough?

*She doesn't answer.*

*Then it comes back, playing on a loop.*

**Duchess** yes. Stop please, I have had enough.

**Ferdinand** sorry. Louder?

**Duchess** yes enough.

**Ferdinand** take away the image, it has done its job

*The Cardinal speaks to Ferdinand.*

**Cardinal** how is the patient?

**Ferdinand** breaking

**Cardinal** not broken?

**Ferdinand** I'll go harder, if that is what you want.

*A bell rings.*

*Ferdinand puts down a cassette recorder.*

**Duchess** what is this now?

*He doesn't answer.*

Ferdinand?

*He presses play.*

no, not Isabella

**Ferdinand** you don't like the sound of your own cub?

**Duchess** where is she?

*Suddenly it snaps off.*

**Ferdinand** just say you are guilty, you accept your crime

**Duchess** please, brother –

**Ferdinand** would you like me to play another one, this is the one where Isabella cries all the harder? Oh and here I have one where she is playing with something that burns her fingers –

*A bell rings.*

**Duchess** you are ill, brother

  these are not the actions of a well person

*More sound and images are thrown at her.*

Ferdinand, where are you?

*A bell rings.*

*Cariola comes in.*

*She brings the Duchess a glass of water.*

**Cariola** they sent you water

**Duchess** you don't have to stay with me

**Cariola** I heard Isabella –

**Duchess** that was his game

**Cariola** no, she is near. That is what they say, in the palace somewhere.

**Duchess** here?

**Cariola** I think so, yes

**Duchess** and alive?

*A bell rings.*

*The video plays again.*

**Duchess**  STOP!

*She stands up. The video stops.*

*A bell rings.*

**Ferdinand**  say you see your mistake. That you were
poisoned by the devil

**Duchess**  I wasn't though, I loved him
*A bell rings.*
*The Duchess walks up and down wringing her hands.*
*She goes to sit again. The video starts up once more.*

*A bell rings.*

**Duchess**  I LOVED HIM

*A bell rings.*

**Cariola**  madam you're distressed

**Duchess**  every time I sit down, look

*She goes to sit, it starts up.*

days without end he has kept this up.

*The images start.*

*A bell rings.*

**Duchess**  I can't sit, I can't sleep
   he wants to torture me.

**Cariola**  but if you don't rest, you'll die –

**Duchess**  no, not death but madness like him.
   Is that it, brother? Have I worked you out?

*A bell rings.*

**Duchess** how mad do you think I will be by the end?

*Then another tune plays.*

*Then another.*


*A bell rings.*

**Duchess** I thought death would be bad, but Cariola madness scares me.

*Then other people start singing it. Rowdy and frightening.*

*Until they are all singing on top of each other.*


*A bell rings.*

**Cardinal** is it done?

**Ferdinand** nearly, she's nearly there


*A bell rings.*

**Duchess** I WON'T BREAK, FERDINAND
I WILL NEVER BREAK


*A bell rings.*

**Cardinal** but is it over?

**Ferdinand** what do you mean, over?

**Cardinal** I mean over over over

*A single guitar note is heard.*

**Duchess**  can you hear that?

*The Duchess steps out of her cell.*

**Cariola**  hang on to sanity, madam

**Duchess**  do you think we shall know one another in the other world?

**Cariola**  who are you talking to?

**Duchess**  I believed I met the dead all around me

**Cariola**  there is no one there

**Duchess**  not in this world but I hear their footsteps
women
I almost see their shape
look, they sit or –

**Cariola**  what do they sing?

**Duchess**  I can't tell, but it seems a song of sorrow
can't you see them?

**Cariola**  no nowhere

**Duchess**  but all around

**Cariola**  ghosts?

**Duchess**  they sing songs of how they came to be free

**Cariola**  how is that?
you said they were dead?

**Duchess**  perhaps not from the past but from tomorrow then

**Cariola**  you are fevered

**Duchess**  yes
I am and in sorrow like I never knew but
will we know when we are dead too?

*Bosola comes in, also standing out of the box.*

**Bosola** I come to build your tomb

**Duchess** so I am right, I am to die?

**Bosola** you know you are.

**Duchess** do you know me –

**Bosola** yes

**Duchess** who am I then?

**Bosola** to the tomb-maker you are worm seed, at best a box of medicine. A little curdled milk, fantastical puff-paste. Feet worn, body weak

**Duchess** who am I to you?

**Bosola** some great woman, sure, for there is turmoil on the forehead, lots of grey hairs, and dying twenty years sooner than she should

**Duchess** you said you knew me –

**Bosola** only as a prison bird
everything I knew before I forgot

**Duchess** I am the Duchess of Malfi
you can't forget that

**Bosola** forgive me, you don't shine like you used to

**Duchess** you speak very plainly

**Bosola** I prefer not to flatter the dead
I am a tomb-maker.

**Duchess** today. Today you are
a while ago you were my horseman

**Bosola** what do you want on your tomb?

**Duchess** that I died twenty years from now, with my

daughter around me

**Bosola** the executioners are early then

**Duchess** shush, did you say that to frighten me, the executioners are here?

**Bosola** I am the common bellman
     that usually is sent to condemn people the night before they suffer

**Duchess** you said you were the tomb-maker?

**Bosola** that was to break it to you gently.

**Duchess** so it is now – my time

**Bosola** I am the bellman, to summons you to death

**Duchess** and soon the undertaker?

**Bosola** yes, that too

**Duchess** you know I know you well
     this game is no defence
     you were my servant, a friend I thought

**Bosola** I was never your servant, I always worked for your brother –

**Duchess** how easily you remove yourself of choice

**Bosola** choice, what choice has a man like me?
     I am the bellman now only, madam, and here's the bell

*A bell rings, they snap back to reality.*

**Cariola** villains, tyrants, murderers! Help! What will you do with my lady? Call for help

**Duchess** what's the point – no one will hear.

**Bosola** remove the maid

**Cariola** I won't go

**Duchess**  no, go, Cariola –

**Cariola**  I'll stay, I'll die with her

**Duchess**  find Isabella and look after her –

**Cariola**  I'll let her be wild and free.

*She is forced out by the two executioners.*

*The Duchess is left with Bosola.*

**Duchess**  how am I to die?

**Bosola**  I told you this business is not my doing

**Duchess**  it is your doing, if you are doing it

**Bosola**  not my design then

**Duchess**  how am I to die?

**Bosola**  that is up to you, if you mean serene –

**Duchess**  serene, how can this be serene?

**Bosola**  quick and easy, no struggle

**Duchess**  I think if we are to honour being alive we
should make it hard

**Bosola**  hard then

**Duchess**  no, easy please
oh hell, I'm frightened now

**Executioners**  we're ready

**Duchess**  might I have a last moment with my daughter
if she is here?
no, I know the answer. Tell her I died bravely then –
I am the Duchess of Malfi still.
I am the Duchess of Malfi still.
I will die like a hero
is this the way you mean to do it?

**Bosola**  yes

95

**Duchess** alright, yes, I see, a rope.

*She backs away. Bosola gets her.*

I am not frightened, don't think I'm frightened
    tell my brothers I wasn't
    I am the Duchess of Malfi still
    but why does the rope scare me so much?
    to be strangled, is it worse than any other way?
    what did I expect, my throat to be opened with
diamonds?
    death is death, however it is delivered.
    tell my brothers, that I was in sound mind,
    this death is the best gift they can give me and that
I can take.

**Executioners** shall we do it, sir?

**Duchess** give my body to my women, after, will you?

**Bosola** yes

**Duchess** yes. I see, the chord goes around my neck
    pull and pull strongly, for your strength must pull
heaven down
    come, violent death
    serve as a potion to make me sleep
    I am the Duchess of Malfi still
    but I die as I was born, Giovanna.
    but wait, wait, one more moment of life –

*They start to strangle her.*

*She struggles.*

*And struggles.*

**Bosola** can't you pull tighter?

**Executioners** we are

**Bosola** tighter still

**Executioners**  she has a strong spirit

**Bosola**  fools, you don't know your art.

*Bosola picks her up.*

*He takes her to a trough of water, and drowns her.*

*She sags.*

*Silence.*

*He wipes the water about himself.*

*Looks at the blood on his hands.*

*Notices the blood on the floor.*

*And the blood on the Duchess.*

*He looks at the Executioners.*

why did she bleed?
   this was a bloodless death

**Executioners**  she hasn't

*Bosola looks at the Executioners.*

**Bosola**  I see blood, clear it up

*A guitar string beats.*

*He looks over.*

did you hear that?

**Executioners**  no

**Bosola**  well, where is the waiting woman?
   somebody else needs to strangle the daughter

*Cariola is brought in.*

**Cariola**  you are damned perpetually for this –
   why should I die?

**Bosola** I am glad you accept that you have to

**Cariola** I do not accept, I won't die

**Bosola** come, dispatch her

**Cariola** I've done nothing wrong

**Bosola** you kept her secret that's what you did

**Cariola** as you keep one for your masters

**Bosola** but bad luck, you will die for it –

**Cariola** you won't kill me, I know you won't

**Bosola** then why am I here holding this rope?

*He shows her the noose of rope.*

**Cariola** let me speak to them then, if they want to accuse me –

**Bosola** they won't like delay, throttle her

**Executioner** she bites and scratches

*She clutches Bosola.*

**Cariola** please, sir
   there is a good man in there, I know there is

**Bosola** don't clutch at me like this

**Cariola** who else can I clutch at?
   if you loved me, even for a second –

*He breaks her neck gently.*

*Both the Duchess and Cariola are dead and at his feet.*

**Bosola** aye.

*He looks at Cariola.*

*He looks at the Duchess.*

**Bosola** she bleeds too.

**Executioner** no?

**Bosola** can't you see it?

**Executioner** perhaps there was something of the witch about them after all.

**Bosola** no witches.

*Bosola looks around.*

**Executioner** the daughter, sir, is dead too as you asked.

*A small child is brought in and put beside her mother.*

*The walls are starting to bleed. The blood pools around their feet.*

**Bosola** why is there so much blood?
    even my own clothes are bleeding –

*He speaks to the Executioner.*

you've done your bit, away

*Ferdinand comes in.*

*He comes over and looks at the Duchess.*

**Ferdinand** cover her face, my eyes are dazzled. It's too bright in here.

*Bosola covers up her face.*

she and I were twins, but now I will always be older.

*He takes the cloth away.*

*He holds the Duchess.*

**Ferdinand** by what authority did you execute her?

**Bosola** what?

**Ferdinand** I just asked by what authority you executed her.

**Bosola** by yours.

**Ferdinand** mine, and was I her judge?

**Bosola** yes, sir.

**Ferdinand** but did any form of actual law condemn her to death? You need a judge and jury for an execution. Did a judge and jury convict her?

**Bosola** now wait –

**Ferdinand** because if not, you bloody fool, you've murdered her –

**Bosola** at your bidding

**Ferdinand** you'll die for it –

**Bosola** you want to tell a court what has happened here?

**Ferdinand** oh I'll tell you how the crime shall be revealed. wolves shall find her, yes packs of them that smell out all butchered corpses, will find her grave and will dig her up not to eat her body, but to tell all that this was MURDER

**Bosola** that you asked for –

**Ferdinand** MURDER MURDER

**Bosola** sir, that you ordered

**Ferdinand** leave me
can we turn the lights down please?

**Bosola** I cannot leave without my payment

**Ferdinand** payment? The only payment you will get is not to be sent to the gallows yourself

**Bosola** but I need no pardon

**Ferdinand**  you're a villain

**Bosola**  when your ingratitude is the judge, I am a villain
but others will call me a servant

**Ferdinand**  your only obedience is to the devil.

**Bosola**  if that is what you call yourself, then yes.
    you have a grave rather than a heart, and your brother
is the same.

**Ferdinand**  is this a man with no heart? Crying for his
sister?

**Bosola**  I feel like I am just waking up out of a dream.
    a nightmare
    oh God, what have I done?
    get away from here

**Ferdinand**  no you get away from here

*He starts to pick up the body of his sister.*

**Bosola**  leave her

**Ferdinand**  she is my sister

**Bosola**  no brother asks for this. Away from her

**Ferdinand**  you don't scare me

**Bosola**  well I should – get out.

*Ferdinand looks frightened for a second. He leaves.*

*Bosola sits with the Duchess's corpse.*

*Beat.*

this is sorrow then

   *He finds the emotion uncomfortable.*

remorse.
    I did this.
    not them, they asked for it but

me.
me.
me.
dear Duchess. I see what I am. I won't hide.
jesus, I won't hide. fucking hell.
scorch me. sun. wind, moon. what have i been?
oh God, hang on, did you –
what, you moved?
come back –
you are warm, still breathing.
Duchess? Take my life, swap with me.
is anyone there? we need some water, something for
her to drink
anything I can do to reverse this I'll do –

*The Duchess stirs.*

**Duchess**  Antonio?

**Bosola**  yes, he's alive
and your son –

**Duchess**  they were shot

**Bosola**  no, the images were made falsely to put pressure
on you.
your husband is alive, and your boy

**Duchess**  they're alive?

**Bosola**  yes, in hiding, we think

**Duchess**  tell them I love them

**Bosola**  stay with me, lady, we'll find them together

**Duchess**  will you tell them?

**Bosola**  no, tell them yourself
no, don't close your eyes
I'll take you there –
madam
your son and husband –

live for them –
please, madam. no.
help
I need help
madam? Can anyone hear

*He tries to resuscitate her.*

please live –

*He tries again.*

*She is dead. He holds her.*

no. no no.

*The Woman with the guitar starts to sing.*

**Woman** (*singing*)
hark now, everything is still
the screech-owl and the whistler shrill
call upon our dame aloud
and bid her quickly don her shroud
strew your hair with powders sweet
don clean linen, bathe your feet
and the foul fiend more to check
a crucifix let bless your neck
'tis now full tide between night and day
end your groan and come away.

*She comes over to the Duchess and cleans off the blood from her.*

*She gives her something warm to wear and dries the water.*

*She does the same to Cariola.*

*And the little girl. The Duchess sits with her*

*Antonio comes on.*

**Antonio**  Delio? Friend, are you here?

*He looks about, can't see anyone.*

Delio –
   I said are you here?

**Duchess**  here

**Antonio**  where?

**Duchess**  where?

**Antonio**  that doesn't sound like you, it sounds like –

**Duchess**  sounds like

**Antonio**  Giovanna?

**Duchess**  Giovanna

**Antonio**  are you there?

**Duchess**  there

**Antonio**  which way do I hear you?

**Duchess**  you

**Antonio**  you're like an echo

**Duchess**  echo

**Antonio**  but an echo is a dead thing
   it sounds like life but has none

**Duchess**  has none

*The Duchess comes very close to Antonio.*

*He feels her.*

*She breathes on him.*

**Antonio**  oh God, you are dead.

*She undoes his shirt and puts her hand inside.*

**Duchess** dead

*He moans with the touch.*

**Antonio** I saw your face a few days ago, on a clear night
presented with sorrow

**Duchess** sorrow

**Antonio** how come you can talk to me?

**Duchess** talk to me

**Antonio** all these months I have feared it, hearing your
death

**Duchess** death

**Antonio** make love to me

**Duchess** love

**Antonio** you're so cold

**Duchess** cold

**Antonio** Giovanna

*Beat.*

don't go.
    I'll kill the bastards that did this to you.
    the fiends.

*Beat.*

no echo there
    is that because we agree?

**Duchess** we agree.
    we agree.

*Delio comes on.*

**Delio** sorry I gor held up –

**Antonio** doesn't matter –

**Delio**  what do you need?

**Antonio**  I have to go tonight, find the Cardinal

**Delio**  tonight?

**Antonio**  she'll help me

**Delio**  who?

*Beat.*

**Antonio**  do you know the way to his rooms?

**Delio**  my wife keeps his key

**Antonio**  your wife?

*Delio hands him the Cardinal's key.*

**Delio**  don't pity me. Plenty men have lost their wives to that piece of vanity. Shall I come with you?

**Antonio**  no, stay here, look after Nico until I come back – would you?

**Delio**  where is he?

**Antonio**  sleeping, but don't wake him yet. I might be back before dawn.

**Delio**  don't get hurt

**Antonio**  I won't

**Delio**  but dear –

**Antonio**  I was a poor excuse for a husband
   I spent all my time wondering how she could love me, rather than loving as fiercely as I should. But now –

**Delio**  you aren't used to fighting –

**Antonio**  I don't care.
   I will try to bring them to justice with words,
   and if words aren't enough

I will use my teeth
and if my teeth aren't enough
I will use my claws
I wasn't born to fight, no. But today I am changed.
I have some strength, don't I? And I have RAGE.


*Cardinal, Doctor and Ferdinand.*

**Cardinal** now, doctor, what's the disease?

**Doctor** a very pestilent disease my lord
they call lycanthropia

**Cardinal** what's that? I need a dictionary to understand
you

**Doctor** in those that suffer there is some melancholy
humour – they imagine themselves to be turned into
wolves.

**Cardinal** what?

**Doctor** observe his movements
he was seen in a churchyard two nights ago, digging a
dead body up

**Cardinal** no

**Doctor** yes, around midnight he was spotted with the
leg of a man on his shoulder, and howling at passers-by
said he was a wolf, and his purpose to sniff out murder

**Cardinal** he said that?

**Doctor** murder he said, yes, murder
don't worry I'll beat the madness out of him
move aside, here he comes

*Ferdinand comes in.*

**Ferdinand** leave me

**Doctor** why does your lordship love to be alone?

**Ferdinand** clever birds fly alone don't they; it's the stupid birds: crows, daws and starlings that flock together

**Doctor** but in the dark –

**Ferdinand** look what's that that follows me?

**Doctor** nothing, my lord

**Ferdinand** yes, there

**Doctor** there is nothing there, just your shadow

**Ferdinand** make it stay, don't let it haunt me

**Doctor** impossible if you move and the sun shines

**Ferdinand** I will throttle it
put the lights down

**Doctor** oh my lord you are angry with nothing

**Ferdinand** you are a fool. How can I catch my shadow unless I fall on it? I need it as a bribe for when I get to hell

**Doctor** get up, good sir

**Ferdinand** I am studying the art of patience

**Doctor** it is a noble virtue

**Ferdinand** shush shush, don't say that, you will scare them all off. Come back
oh, where's it gone, you've made it go – I can't lose it, we have work to do

**Cardinal** get him up

*They get Ferdinand to his feet.*

**Ferdinand** use me well, you were best: what I have done –
what have I done? Have I done something? I won't

confess –

**Doctor**  are you mad, my lord? Are you out of your wits?

**Ferdinand**  who's he?

**Cardinal**  your doctor

**Ferdinand**  that's not a doctor, doctors have beards –

**Doctor**  if you come here, we have a little remedy

**Ferdinand**  a remedy? hide me from him: doctors are like kings, they think they are always right
   get away away

**Doctor**  now he's frightened of me, leave us alone

**Cardinal**  take your gown off

**Doctor**  no, I need my gown, this cure can be a messy business. Let me have forty syringes full of medication, and straps and a cloth he can bite down

**Cardinal**  what?

**Doctor**  you treat the mad with a firm hand if you want results

**Ferdinand**  you are cruel, doctor, I know how you play with me? I will stamp you into a stew, pull off your skin and show your skeleton

**Doctor**  stop your dancing, man, we will have no more of it here
   there is nothing I haven't seen

**Ferdinand**  get the doctor away from me, he makes me worse

*The Doctor uses a cattle-prod on Ferdinand, who recoils.*

**Doctor**  what has happened before this began?

**Cardinal**  nothing

**Doctor**  some trauma or sudden grief?

**Cardinal**  he said he saw a ghost, I didn't believe him

**Doctor**  a ghost –?

**Cardinal**  a woman, so he said

**Doctor**  which woman?

**Cardinal**  do you think it is possible?

**Doctor**  I believe he may think it is. Who was the woman?

**Cardinal**  no one important

**Doctor**  he mentions his sister –

**Cardinal**  our sister has gone on a long trip, he misses her. But she's not the ghost

**Doctor**  I'll cure him. Do you have any restrictions on my methods?

**Cardinal**  none.

**Doctor**  good. Expect results.

*He uses the cattle-prod, and takes Ferdinand off.*

*The Cardinal is alone for a second. He thinks he sees something too.*

*The ghosts play with him for a second.*


*Julia comes in.*

**Julia**  have you heard it?

**Cardinal**  could you knock

**Julia**  some are saying that your sister is missing

**Cardinal**  my sister?

**Julia** the Duchess yes

**Cardinal** she is on a pilgrimage

**Julia** but she never arrived
Four years she has been gone and never seen

*Beat.*

aren't you worried? The world is ablaze with this news.

**Cardinal** not worried no.

**Julia** where is she?

**Cardinal** my sister will be doing her own thing, somewhere. I don't see treachery like you do.
why did you come here tonight?

**Julia** me?

**Cardinal** yes

**Julia** to see you.

*She comes over and kisses him.*

because I heard the whispers of concern about the
Duchess and I thought . . .

**Cardinal** women and tittle-tattle

**Julia** maybe she married some nobleman and is living in
Paris

**Cardinal** maybe she did

**Julia** or went somewhere to a convent after her mourning

**Cardinal** indeed

**Julia** or some other explanation that leaves her happy.

*She tries to sit on his lap.*
*He pushes her away.*

**Cardinal**  better that you hadn't come tonight

**Julia**  so you are worried?

**Cardinal**  do you believe in ghosts, Julia?

**Julia**  the church says no

**Cardinal**  exactly
the church says no, I say no

**Julia**  do you know where she is?

**Cardinal**  what if I were to say all around me?

**Julia**  what?

**Cardinal**  the only way to keep you quiet is to say
nothing, get out of here

**Julia**  if you know something you must tell them

**Cardinal**  I don't need your interrogation

**Julia**  no interrogation
but aren't we in this together? We are already damned
by our adultery after all

**Cardinal**  what if I tell you and you find the secret is like
poison? Once you have heard it, you can't unhear

**Julia**  is it so bad?

**Cardinal**  my sister is dead

**Julia**  what happened to her?

**Cardinal**  strangled

**Julia**  oh God

**Cardinal**  by my appointment and that of my brother

**Julia**  I don't believe you

**Cardinal**  believe it

**Julia** for what crime?

**Cardinal** adultery.

**Julia** like us

**Cardinal** yes
and her young daughter was also strangled.

**Julia** oh heaven. Sir.

**Cardinal** you see?
it's easier to tie knots than to untie them.

**Julia** why?

**Cardinal** what, that is all you can say why? That settles
this? Why why?
because she wouldn't be obedient.
because she wouldn't learn.
can your bosom take that? We killed her.

**Julia** would you kill me for the same crime? Adultery

**Cardinal** fuck off

**Julia** what difference is your sister and me?

**Cardinal** I don't care about you.
that's the difference.

*Beat.*

**Cardinal** oh stop it, don't pout, I've told you now

**Julia** everyone is looking for her

**Cardinal** so tell them.
in fact yes tell them. You would love that.
you are in a position Julia to bring this all to an end
for me.
tell them.
she is buried under her basement, let them find her
there.

    I am tired of my conscience, it sits like lead in my
bosom

**Julia**  I will tell them

**Cardinal**  good. Swear you will, I need deliverance

**Julia**  most religiously

*He takes out a Bible.*

**Cardinal**  kiss it

**Julia**  must I kiss it?

**Cardinal**  yes, kiss it

*He takes her head and gets her to kiss it*
*She does so.*

**Cardinal**  –you would do this, I see it now.

**Julia**  I would, sir

*He takes her by the neck and dashes her head on the table.*

**Cardinal**  how tedious is a guilty conscience.
    how tedious. Julia.

*He looks at the ghost.*

and you can stop too

*Bosola enters.*

ha Bosola, very well
    now you know me for your fellow murderer –
    it's alright, she has gone. Another for the grave

**Bosola**  how can you say that?

**Cardinal**  how can I, says he who also has murder as his
trade?

**Bosola**  do you know where Antonio is?

**Cardinal**  what do you want with him? Help me move

this body first

**Bosola** I have a message from the Duchess

**Cardinal** tsspp.
  what, that you mean to deliver, what, all kisses and –
  she's dead and you're a murderer, you can't change

**Bosola** even a murderer can do something good

**Cardinal** don't do that

**Bosola** what?

**Cardinal** I have a call from chief of justice this morning
who said you are still wanted
  I didn't know that you had escaped your ship

*Beat.*

**Bosola** I won't go back

**Cardinal** and I will help you in that
  but look at yourself
  be realistic, the soul is formed in childhood and yours
is twisted

**Bosola** where is he?

*Beat.*

**Cardinal** I will tell you if you swear allegiance still to me

**Bosola** I work for your brother now

**Cardinal** okay, my brother, yes, okay
  you are my brother's now, yes?

*Beat.*

are you loyal to him?

*Beat.*

**Bosola** as long as he pays me – I am loyal

**Cardinal** good. I'll tell you where Antonio is
you can deliver your message by all means, then do my bidding.
there is a man called Delio. A slight man, inconsequential man.
I knew his wife –
Antonio is staying with him.
lure them to some quiet place and there use this, you can say what you want before you kill him.

*He gives Bosola a gun.*

and Bosola, dear sweet boy
you can't shrug off your past as easily as you might like

*He leaves.*

*Bosola holds the gun.*

**Bosola** I must look to my footing
in such slippery ice pavements men may break their necks
this is new ground for me.
how this man bears up in blood, seems fearless.
will I bear up too when it comes to the moment?
soul untwist and – penitence, let me fully drink from your cup

**Duchess** that throws men down only to raise them up.

*He looks around.*

**Bosola** Duchess is that you?


*Ferdinand walks in. Subdued. And wearing the Duchess's dress.*

*The Cardinal in a flap, trying to get ready.*

**Cardinal** for God's sake

change into a suit.

*Ferdinand sits down without doing so.*

we must appear as worried brothers this evening.
  get out of that daft attire.
  she's gone

*He looks at Ferdinand.*

a suit, brother.
  the doctor says it is only in dark that you are mad, so
here – here is some light

*He shines a light in his eyes.*

*Ferdinand howls from the pain.*

there is much interest in her whereabouts.
  you understand what this means? Everyone is looking
for her, and we must be amongst that.
  are you even listening now, brother?

*He looks at Ferdinand.*

quickly change.
  we must mourn her and talk about our grave concern.
  you have to get yourself in tune and quickly we have
to be seen to be together and distraught.
  we are in danger. Idiot boy, and shame on me that I
ever listened to you. We are in the middle of a nightmare
of our own creation
  cure yourself, if there is any of you left?
  dance out of this.
  change

**Ferdinand**  villain

**Cardinal**  oh, so you still speak?
  good, you can speak more. You can tell the world of
her gentle nature and how terribly worried we are for her
welfare

*Ferdinand spits at him.*

why do that?
    it was you who brought this all about.

*Ferdinand bites the Cardinal.*

*The Cardinal uses the cattle-prod.*

the doctor says I should use this on you every time you
show your teeth. So –
    if you are a wild animal now then

**Ferdinand** watch out watch out

**Cardinal** what?

**Ferdinand** that instrument is only borrowed, the doctor
will come and when the doctor comes –

**Cardinal** stop this fucking madness, you don't fool me

*Ferdinand lunges at the Cardinal and bites him.*

*The Cardinal fights back.*

*Ferdinand rips at his face.*

*Half his face is hanging off.*

what have you done?

**Ferdinand** the doctor, the doctor will mend it. With a rod
and a stick and a boiling hot pan of fancies and –

*The Cardinal gets the cattle-prod.*

*He uses it on Ferdinand.*

*Ferdinand shrieks.*

they want to talk to the family
    I am the family
    then let us talk, oh, we have much to say about how
we killed our sister

*The Cardinal uses the cattle-prod again.*

**Ferdinand** our sister our sister our sister

*The Cardinal uses it again.*

our sister our sister

*The Cardinal uses it again and again and again.*

our sister

*And again.*

*It's horrible and too much for a person to take.*

*Ferdinand is still.*

**Cardinal** I'll sit alone then.
  I will tell the world how much she is missed and how
keen we are to have her home.

*He goes over and kicks Ferdinand.*

*Bosola enters with Antonio.*

**Bosola** I found him, sir

**Cardinal** but only done half your task
  I see
  my brother's madness has meant I have sent my
servants away.
  come in, dear Antonio, how nice to finally meet you.

**Antonio** your office is full of corpses

**Cardinal** that isn't a corpse, just my brother isn't feeling
well
  see, he vomits.

*He puts a cloth over him.*

I'm glad to see you actually, with all this concern about
my sister's whereabouts I am sure you will be much

questioned

**Antonio**  I will be questioned?

**Cardinal**  yes, it seems we have a marriage contract with your name on it, so if you were in contact with her, you'll find the cloud of suspicion hanging around your shoulders

**Antonio**  how dare you?

**Cardinal**  I don't think it is a question of dare
my sister could be in grave danger
and you were possibly the last to see her

**Antonio**  I haven't seen her for a long time

**Cardinal**  so you say, but really any one of us could say that

**Antonio**  you killed her

**Cardinal**  Bosola, I believe you have a task, could you do it?

**Bosola**  what task is that, master?

*The Cardinal looks from one to another.*

**Cardinal**  the task we mentioned and I equipped you for

**Bosola**  that is lost from my memory, sir

**Antonio**  you killed my wife

**Cardinal**  oh, your wife –

**Antonio**  it doesn't matter if you deny it

**Cardinal**  and what if I did? She was my family

**Antonio**  she belonged to none of us

**Cardinal**  don't tell me you have come to avenge,
but let me enjoy this for a minute. By what means?

a frown. A few mean words?
  have you got a pen you can dash at me?

*He laughs.*

dispatch him, would you, Bosola, enough of this

**Bosola** no

**Cardinal** what?

**Bosola** I won't

**Cardinal** very good, but do as I say

**Bosola** I think for myself now

**Cardinal** what, you are crawling from the gutter and
becoming a rat rather than a worm?
  kill him

*Bosola hands Antonio the gun.*

**Bosola** this pistol was meant for your end, Antonio, now
use it to bring his

*Antonio's hand is shaking.*

**Cardinal** no.

**Bosola** he has taken everything from you.

**Cardinal** put it down

**Bosola** pull it quickly, it's best done fast

*Antonio looks to Bosola.*

a quick movement does it, do it

**Antonio** I can't

**Cardinal** he hasn't the guts

**Bosola** just pull your finger

**Antonio** my finger won't pull

**Bosola** squeeze

**Cardinal** you see, he can't even with instruction –

*Antonio pulls the trigger.*

*The Cardinal falls down dead.*

*Antonio looks in disbelief.*

**Bosola** well done

**Antonio** that came from me?

**Bosola** yes

**Antonio** and he, is he dead?

**Bosola** yes, I think, dead

**Antonio** I never want to hold this thing again

**Bosola** put it down then

**Antonio** he's moving still

**Bosola** twitching but –

**Antonio** shall I shoot him again to be sure?

**Bosola** I think it's done

**Antonio** his eyelids are flickering

**Bosola** this is the after-moments only.
his spirit is gone

**Antonio** a black cloud then around the room

**Bosola** the pair of them

**Antonio** it's funny, when I shot him I got this jolt of being alive

**Bosola** this is not a life you want

**Antonio** let me shoot again

**Bosola**  no, this is once only, your nature is gentle. throw the gun away.

**Antonio**  I don't want to

**Bosola**  put it down.

**Antonio**  I can't

*He holds the gun up.*

I think I see her all around me everywhere she watches

**Bosola**  then show her that your nature is not changed.

*He comes over and takes the gun from Antonio, throwing it across the room.*

good men don't need guns and knives. They persuade and lead, not force and bully.

*Ferdinand revives.*

**Ferdinand**  strangling is a very quiet death what say to that? Whisper softly, do you agree to it?

**Bosola**  sir?

*Ferdinand picks up the gun.*

**Ferdinand**  strangle me

**Antonio**  what?

*He plays with it from one hand and another.*

**Ferdinand**  or drown me perhaps like you did my sister?

*He shoots Antonio.*

**Bosola**  oh God.

**Ferdinand**  I didn't mean it. please sir, I don't want the doctor to see. He makes me cry. And he says for all the wealth in Europe he shouldn't –

*The gun goes off again.*

*Bosola is hit in the leg.*

**Bosola**  arrgghhh
  put it down

**Ferdinand**  don't tell the doctor –

**Bosola**  put the weapon down

**Ferdinand**  yes, for the doctor mustn't know. Oh but it hurt my thumb, my thumb is sore, who will comfort it now she has gone?
  who will sing to me when I am scared?
  oh drown me pretty please, sir

**Bosola**  drown?
  no

**Ferdinand**  yes dunk me like you did my sister

**Bosola**  I want you to feel as bad as I do.
  to shake with regret and remorse

*Ferdinand puts the gun to his own head.*

please sir, no more

*Ferdinand shoots.*

*He falls down dead.*

*Bosola is surrounded by bodies.*

*His leg is a mess, he can't walk on it.*

*He moves over to Antonio.*

sir
  is there anything of your life left?
  sir?

*Antonio stirs slightly.*

**Antonio** this is my after-twitching like you said
   it was you who killed her?

**Bosola** yes sir. No, no no

*Antonio is dead.*

Duchess, I would have given my life to save his
   you must know that
   where are you?
   if I take my knife and use it, will that be an end,
Duchess?

*He takes his knife.*

*He puts the knife to his throat.*

*He closes his eyes.*

*He hesitates.*

it seems I don't have the courage you had at your death

*He tries again.*

*He holds the knife up.*

*He tries to slash himself.*

*He can't do it.*

*He painfully goes over and picks up Ferdinand's gun.*

*He holds it to his head.*

*He closes his eyes.*

what is this?
   why can't I do it?

*His arms starts to shake.*

Duchess, is this your final trick?
   are you laughing at me now?

*He tries one final time.*

every single thing I ever did I got wrong

*He tries again.*

*He finally fires it.*

*It's a blank.*

*It doesn't work. He tries again. Blank.*

*Delio runs in.*

sir, you come too late

**Delio**  what has happened?

**Bosola**  all dead, and one more coming –

**Delio**  no, sir. Stop.

**Bosola**  I am no one, and not a sir.

**Delio**  whoever you are, stop, no more death. But what, not Antonio –?

**Bosola**  yes

**Delio**  no, not Antonio, no no –

*Delio comes and holds Antonio's body.*

*Bosola watches.*

*Delio cries.*

this was my best friend, and the best of men.
    he never knew how much I loved him.

*He looks up.*

what will I do with the child?

**Bosola**  what child?

**Delio**  the boy outside, Nico

**Bosola**  take him away, this is no place for children

**Delio**  but what do I do with him?
  he is the duke but will anyone believe, he was born in
secret and unseen

**Bosola**  he must be raised to know how great his parents
were

**Delio**  I am in so much debt that I am wanted for prison
myself

**Bosola**  too bad

**Delio**  I will take him to an institution

**Bosola**  an institution, no, not if you loved his father

**Delio**  I will take him to the doors of the church then

**Bosola**  no, that was what happened to me, it can't
happen again

**Delio**  well you suggest another way

**Bosola**  Antonio was your friend

**Delio**  as the Duchess was yours

**Bosola**  not really, only at the very end

**Delio**  I can't do it

**Bosola**  what does that look mean?

**Delio**  you're free, aren't you, you can walk under the
sky?

**Bosola**  I doubt I will even walk at all if I even survive
this –

**Delio**  take all the possessions I have on me
  I am in a dead end. I don't want to take the boy into
that with me

**Bosola**  you understand what courage is?

**Delio**  enough to know I have none

*He takes a watch and a crucifix out of his pockets and throws it at Bosola.*

**Bosola**  stop
   no I won't take it, I –

*Delio walks away.*

wait.

*The boy walks in.*

no, wait
   don't look at them.
   stand there. Okay.

*He painfully finds a way to stand up, and covers the bodies with a cloth.*

we'll find a nice woman to raise you
   there must be many in this place
   or a convent
   yes, with nuns.
   don't cry.
   or cry if you need, but then –

*He looks at the child.*

*The child looks at him.*

I cannot help you.
   I cannot help myself, so how could I help you?
   Duchess. if this is you, know I can't help this.
   I cannot raise a child.
   I was no good as a man. I was the worst of men.
   I understood too late the greatness in women.
   and I utterly missed the value of love.

*The boy comes over to him.*

I can't do it, sweet boy.

there is nowhere to go for you and me.

*The room starts to shift.*

*The ghosts create a room that looks more modern.*

Duchess?

*The Duchess steps behind Bosola with a glass of milk.*

*She puts it in his hand.*

*The boy comes and takes the glass of milk.*

*And drinks it.*

**Duchess** these wretched things will leave no more behind them than falling in a frost leaves a print in snow: as soon as the sun shines, it melts away.

**Bosola** we won't forget

**Duchess** take my boy's hand.

**Bosola** please –

**Duchess** my boy's hand.

*He takes the boy's hand.*

and change it.